HAIKU: IN VENICE

HAIKU: OF ANCIENT FUTURES

HAIKU: A GARDEN

CAROLINE GAY WAY : OKOME

MORE STORIES, ART, POETRY AND VIDEO SHORTS CAN BE
FOUND ON CAROLINE'S WEBSITE:

WWW. CAROLINEWAY.CO.UK

To Hermione, Venice-Vivienne and Caroline Wiseman

Contents

HAIKU: IN VENICE

Adrift in time - meandering through Venice backwaters in twisting shadowed byways

HAIKU: OF ANCIENT FUTURES

Timeless Japanesque fragments of human interaction entwined with nature - sometimes delivered with a futuristic twist

HAIKU: A GARDEN

Moments of life from Spring days in Aldeburgh Sensory Garden

a gondola breaks
the summer moon reflection
gliding on ripples

beside a moss path
a box has been delivered
dripping in the rain

sensory garden notes
whispering flowers nodding
strum the gentle breeze

HAIKU IN VENICE

Adrift in time — meandering through Venice backwaters in twisting shadowed byways

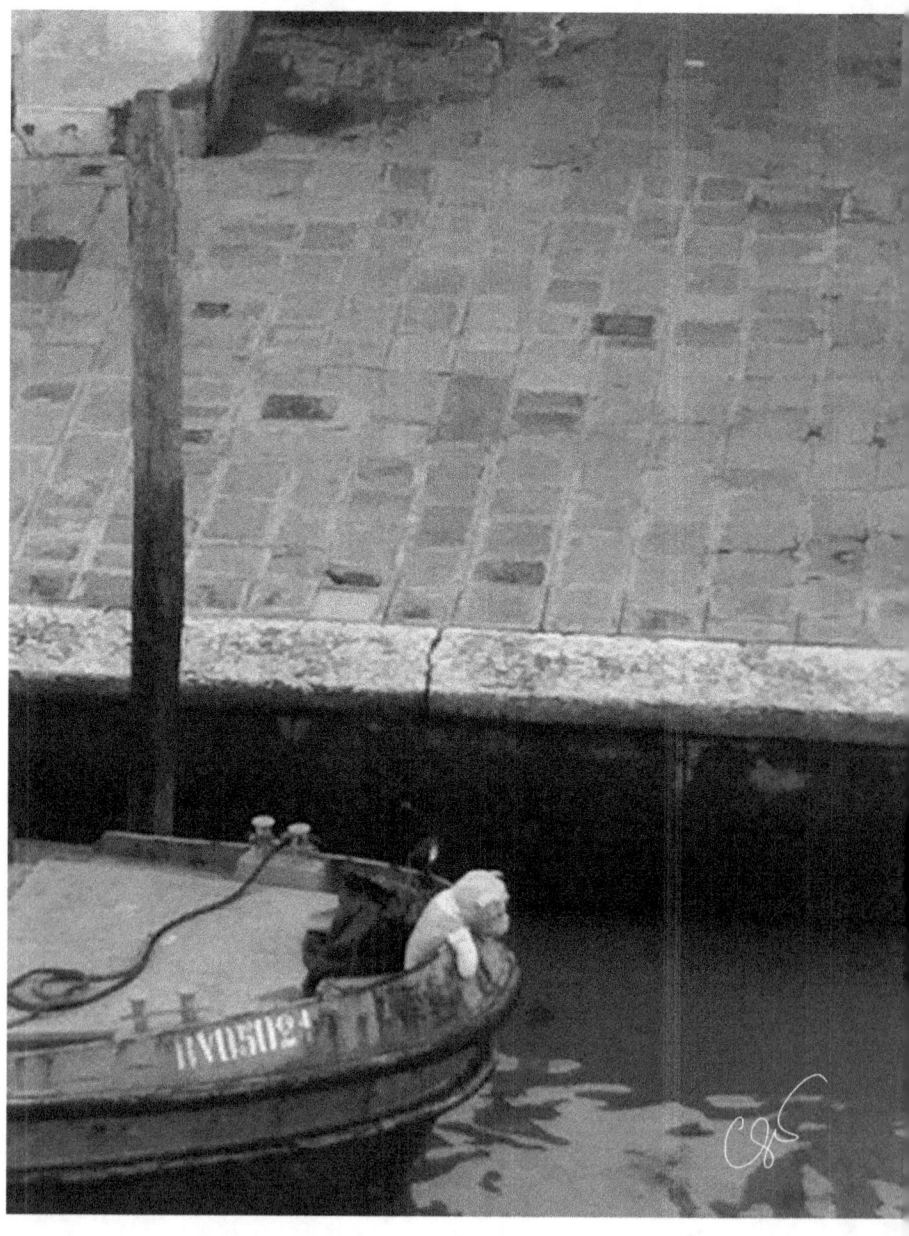

an old toy bear stares
into the depths at dawn
from a Venice bin boat

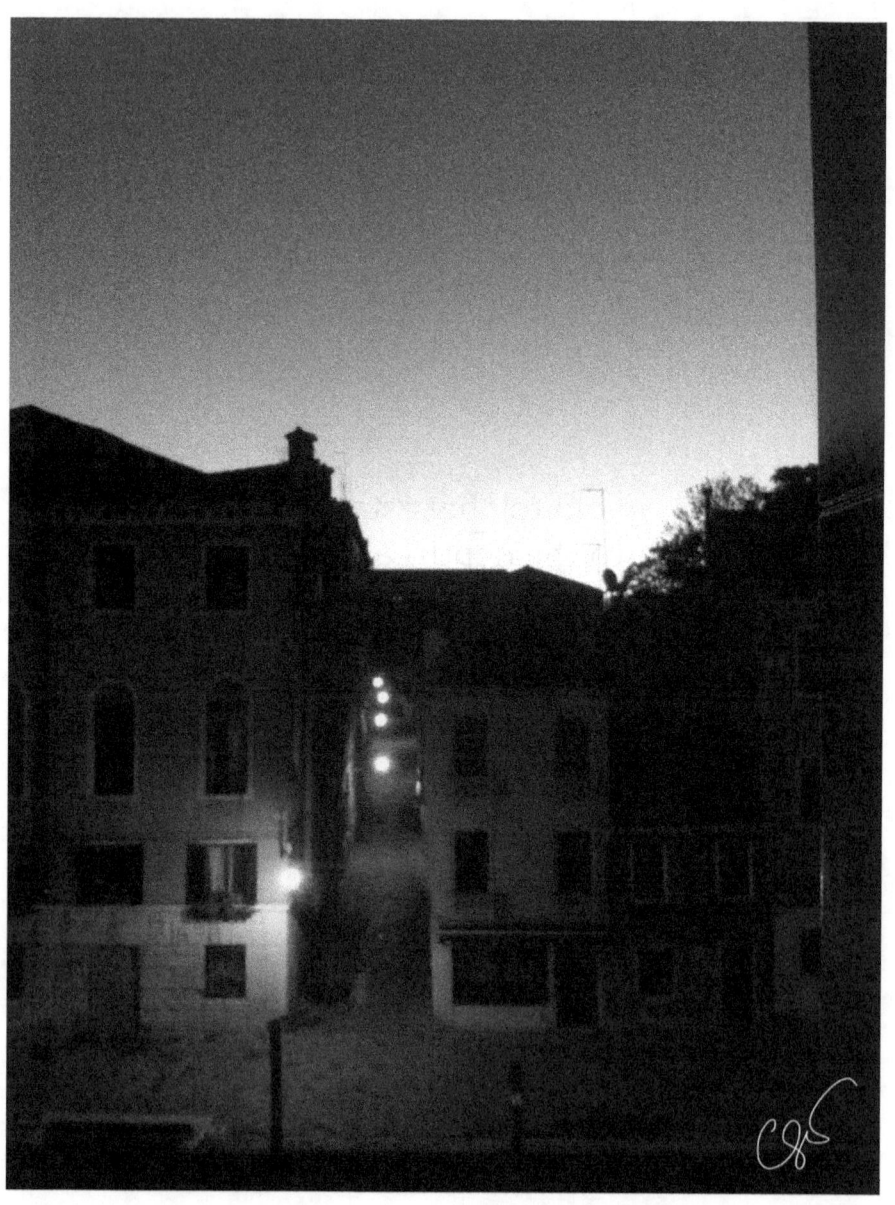

above a working canal
cool summer dawn foreshadows
the lights going out

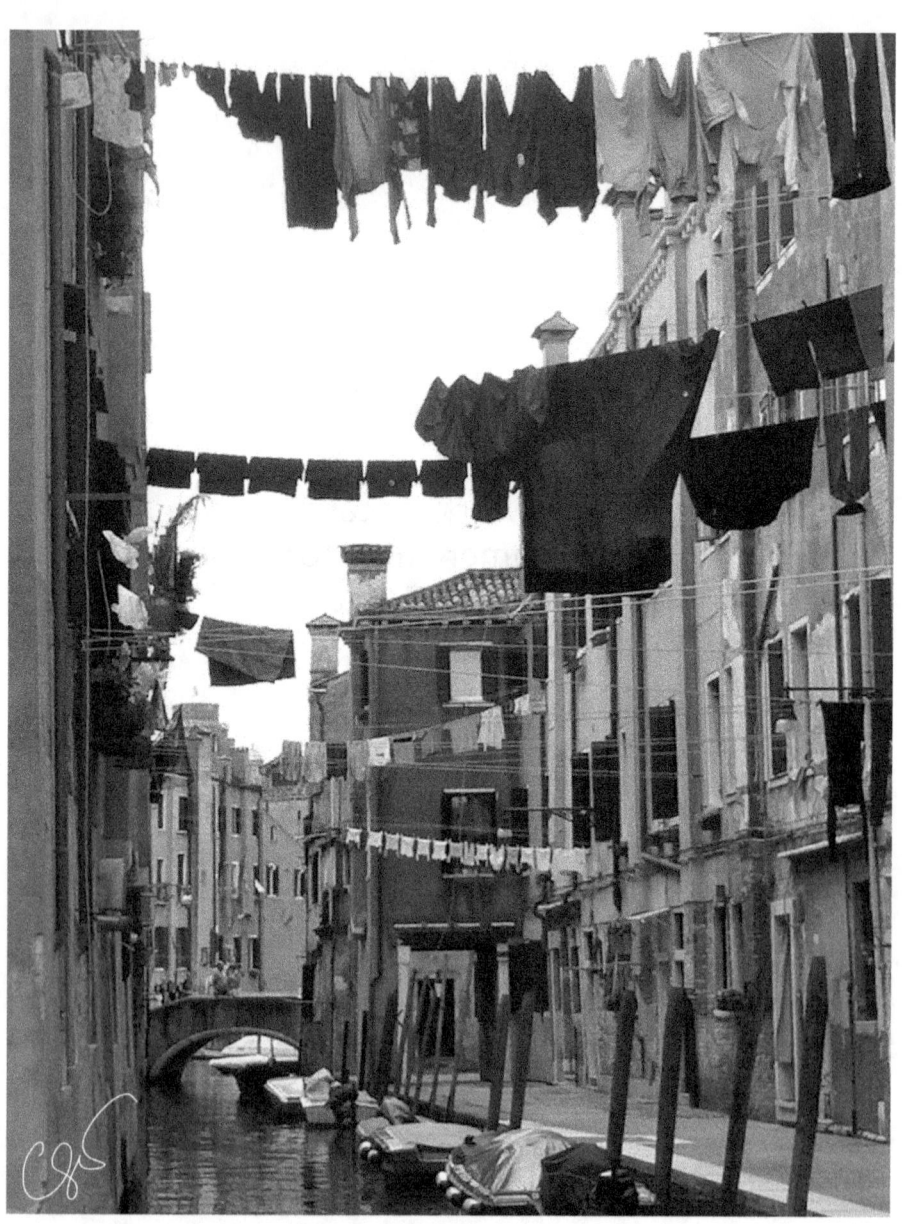

washing lines string out
across dark water each one
a family of flags

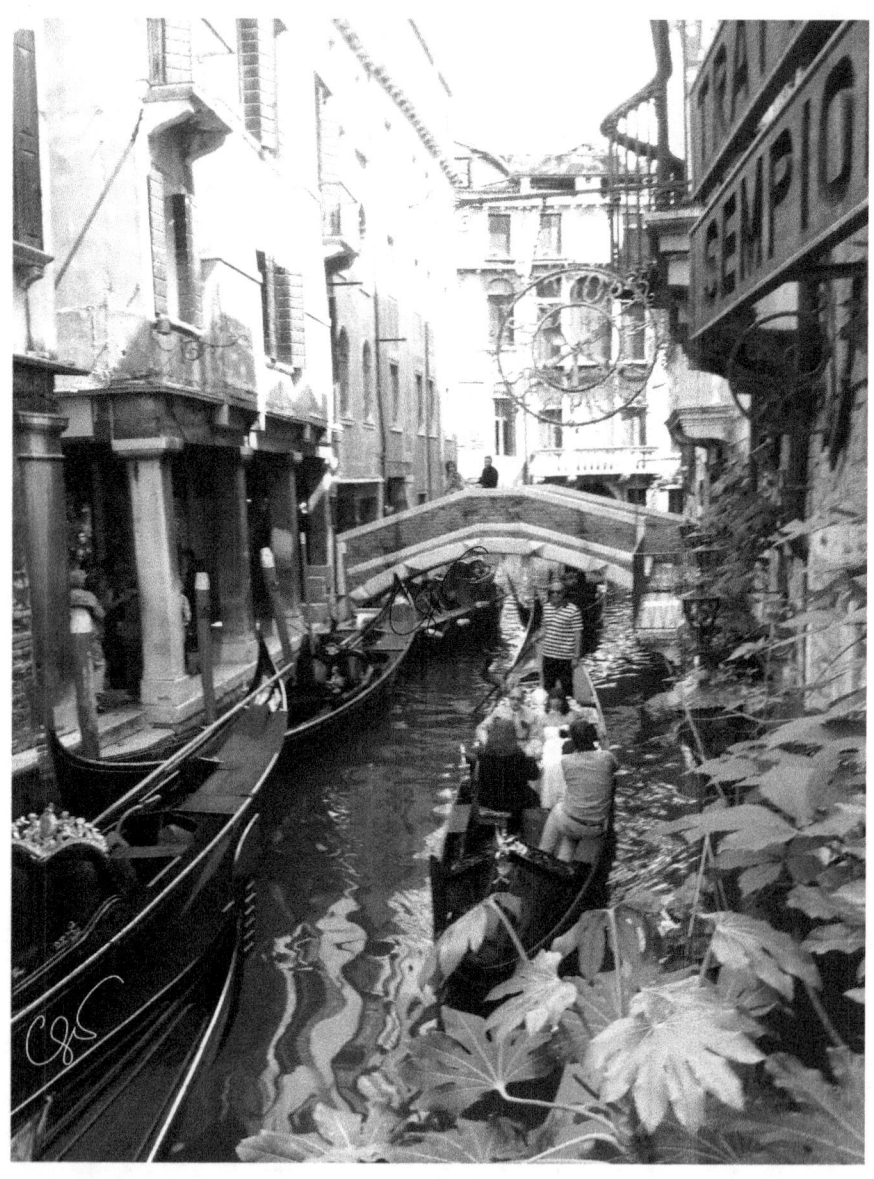

leaves and flowers cling
silently above canals
as tourists chatter

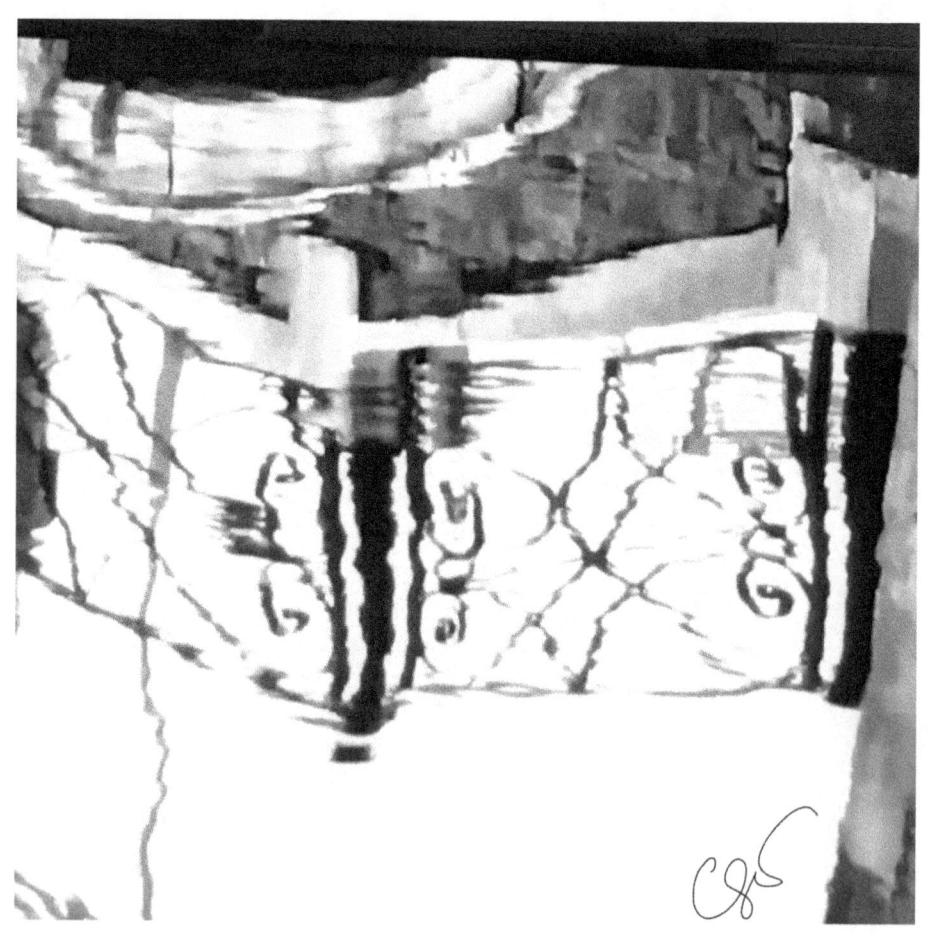

under a stone bridge
wisps of an old serenade
floating echoes glide

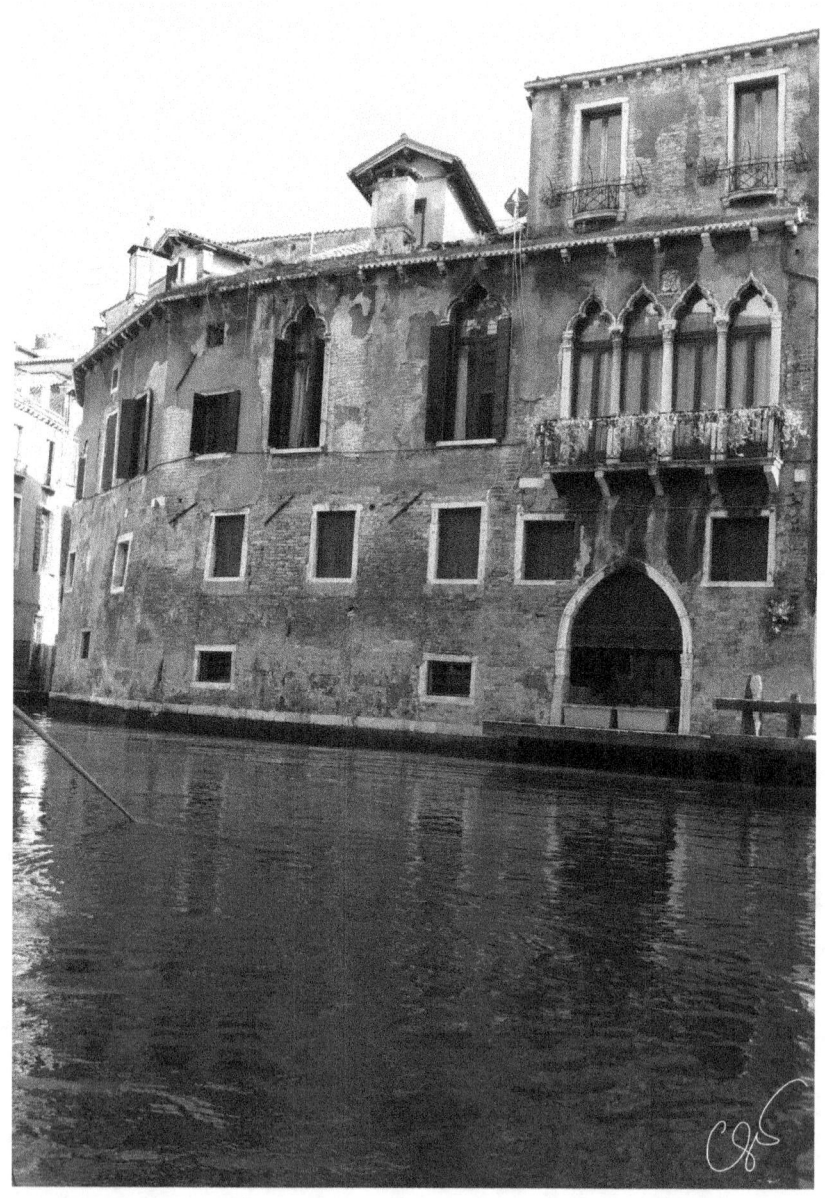

through white gauze curtains
light ripples on the ceiling
a gondolier sings

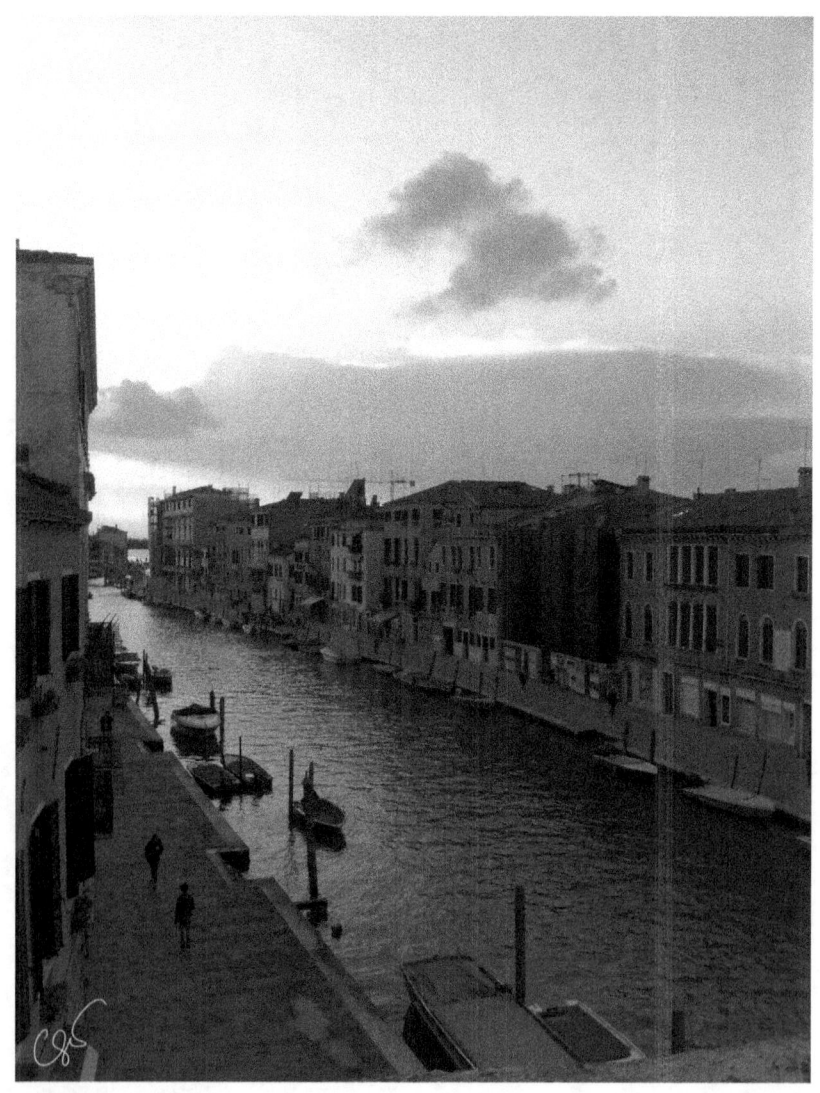

for a few early hours
the waterways are wrapped
in perfect silence

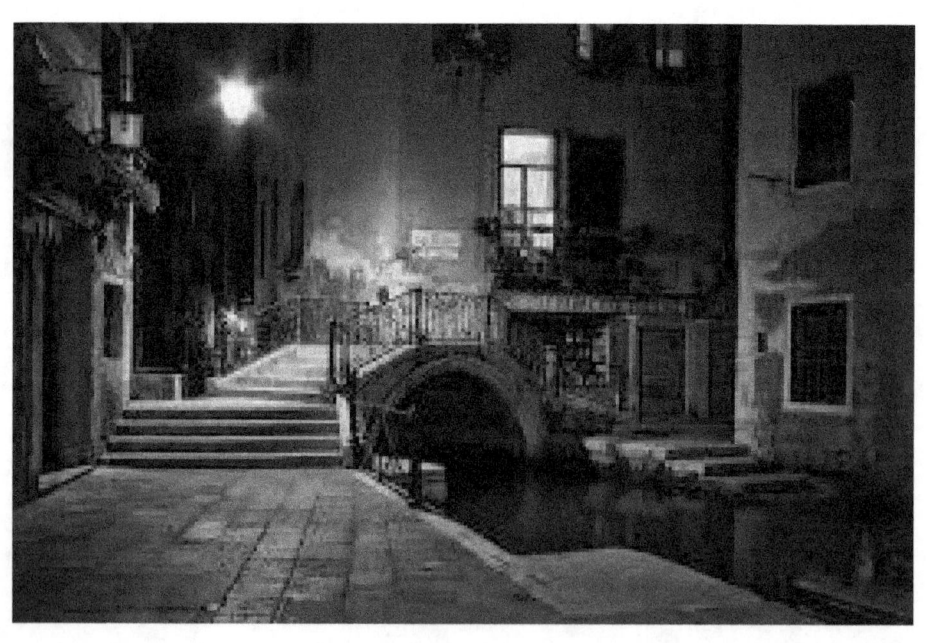

on a back street bridge
echoes of late night footsteps
disturb dusty webs

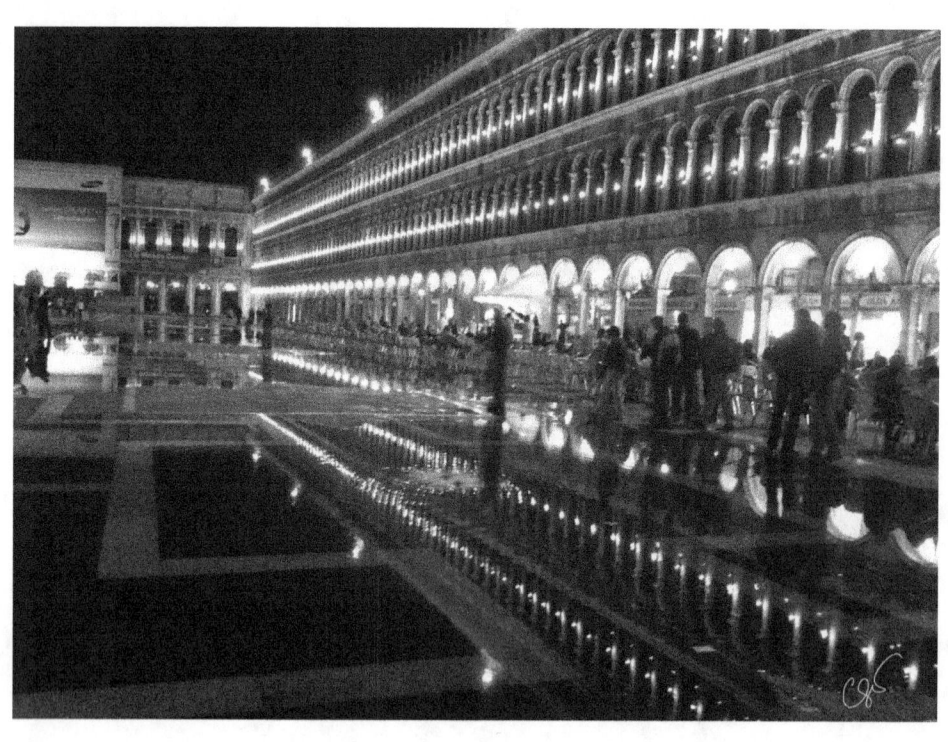

St Mark's Square floods
as evening waters rise to
tourist's mute surprise

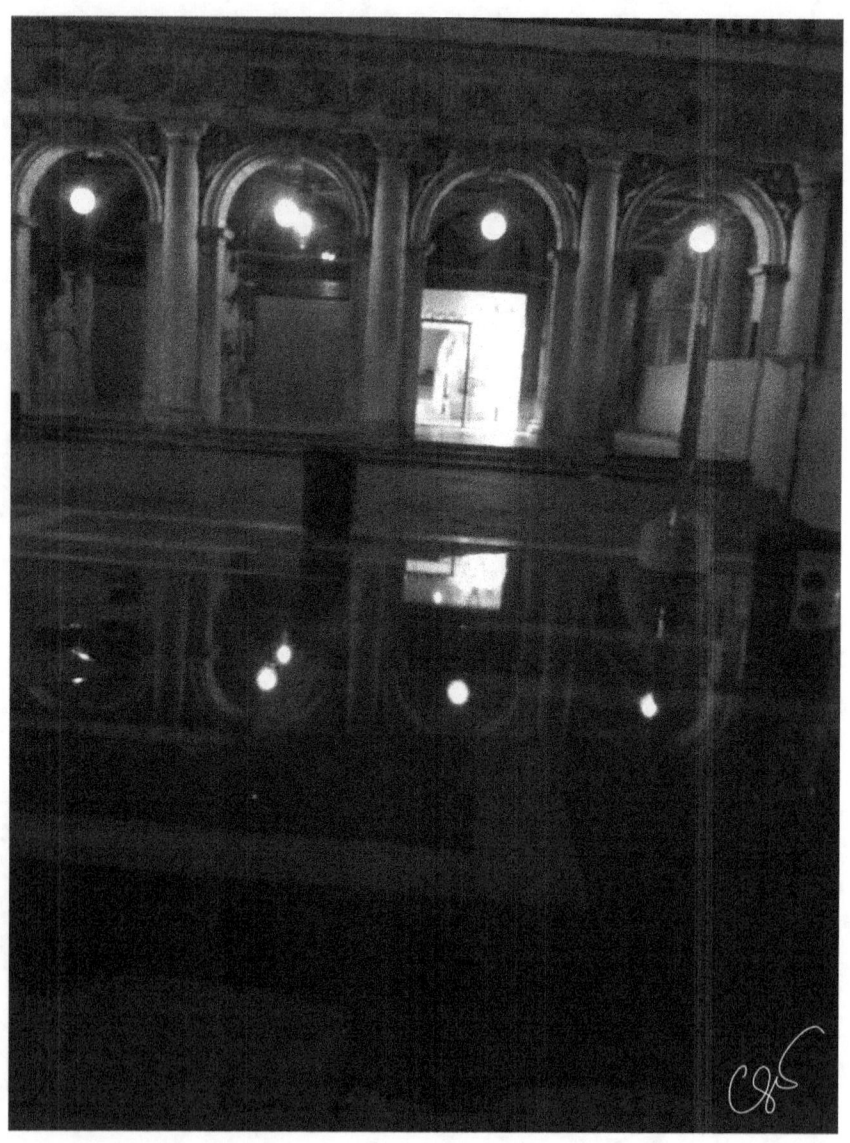

modern light reflects
the ancient city sinking
back into the mud

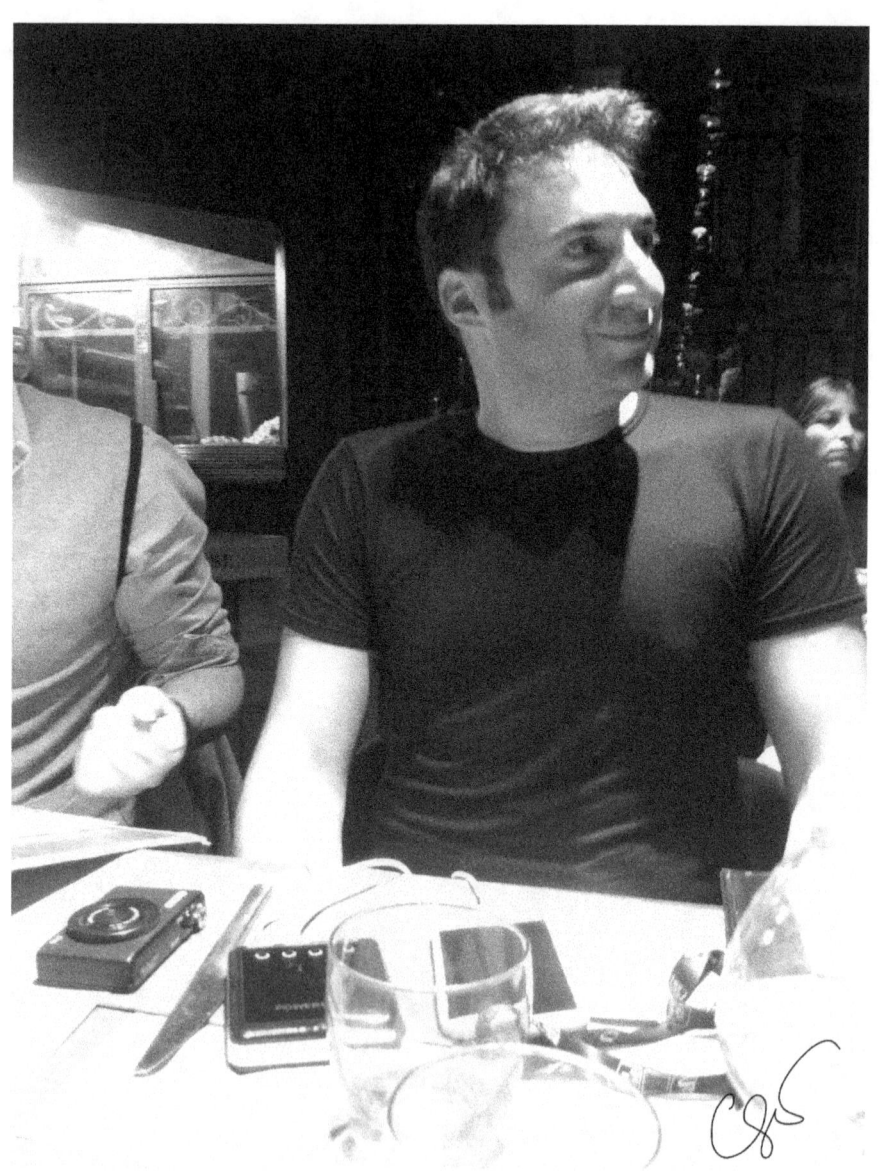

having lunch with a
venetian entrepreneur
is electronic sushi

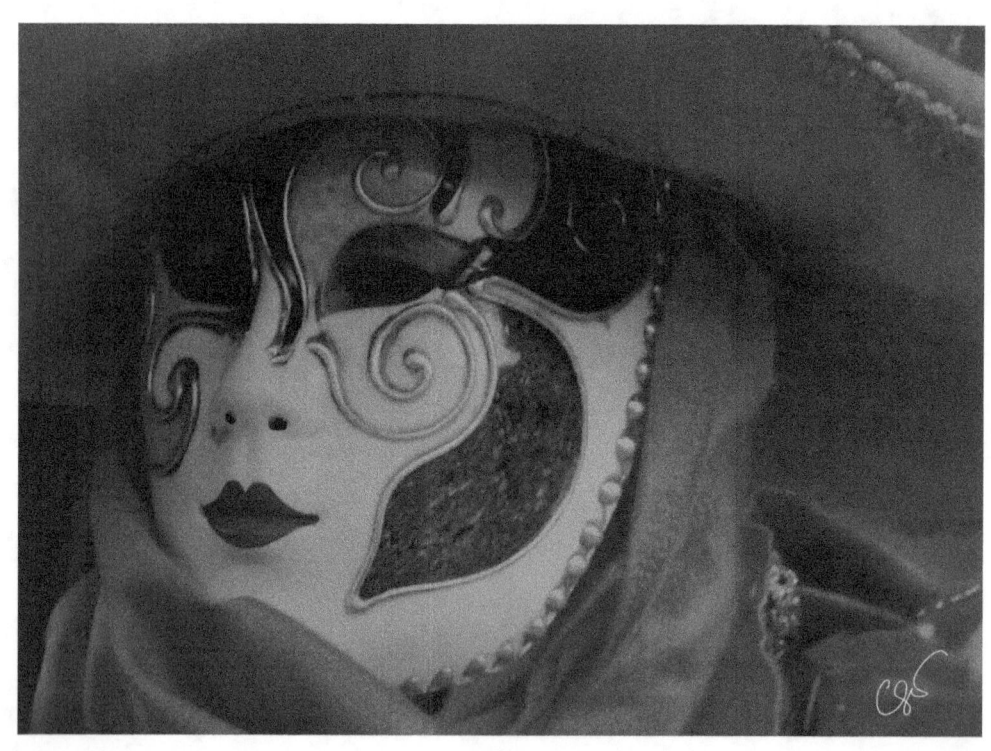

a forgotten mask
afloat in a dawn canal
drowns in bright sunlight

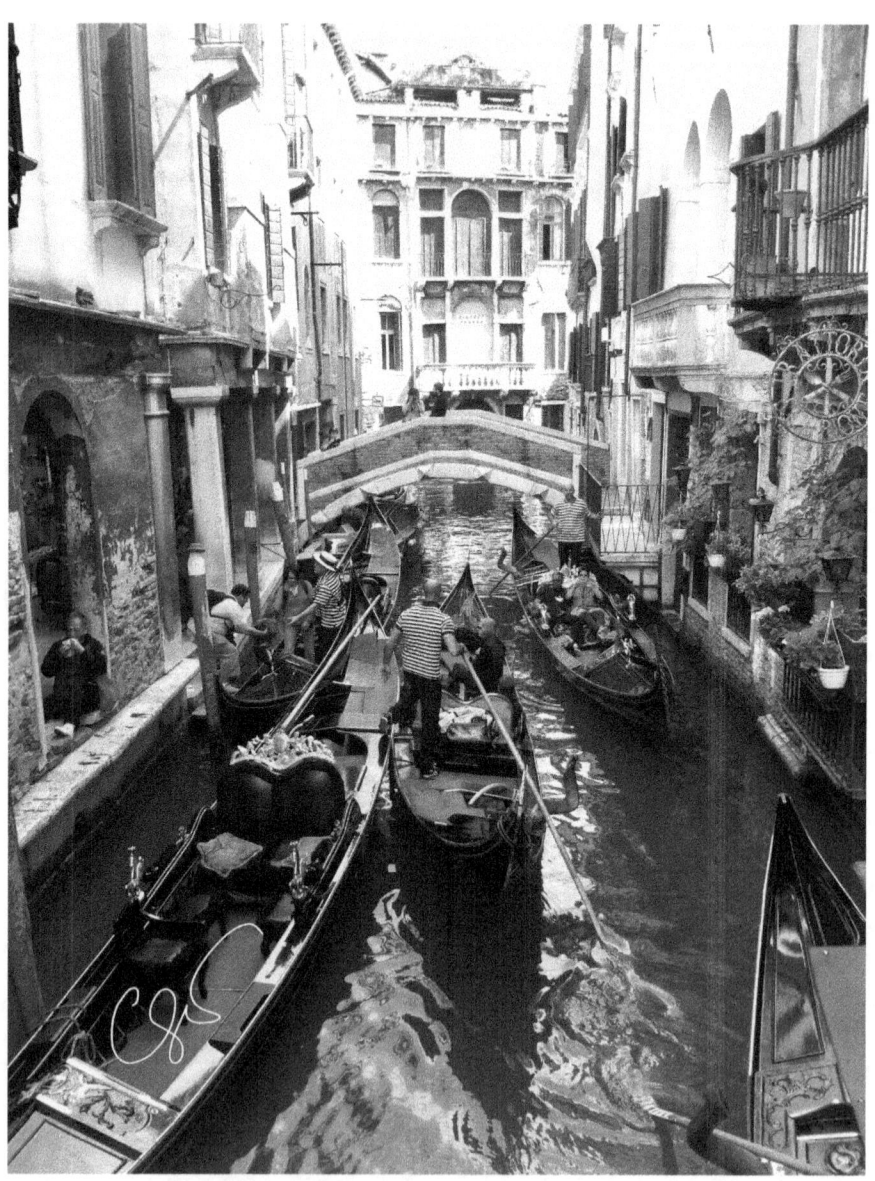

in a dark archway
walls echo with floating crowds
as an old man eats

unseen by revellers
a spider caught in darkness
bounces on it's web

Vivaldi's 'Seasons'
flow through timeless Venice
to dance in fire waves

in a backwater canal
jazz and coffee mingle
in late morning air

eyes shine moonlight
entwined with Casanova
in Venice waterways

drinking of moonshine
in a midsummer nights dream
workmen saunter home

water-light shimmers
around a dusty crevice
an old web trembles

long fingers trailing
send liquid sunbursts swirling
from her languid hand

a merchant of Venice
passes an English playwright
his goose quill in hand

with maps and purpose
young Marco strides across the square
in his new made shoes

a gondola breaks
the summer moons reflection
softening ripples repair

as dawn breaks
a mask-maker strides to his shop
listening to birdsong

beside the canal
taste Scampi alla Veneziana
water reflects the moment

beside a canal
in the forgotten wine glass
a moth drowns

bathed in streetlamp shadow
wine from Tre Venezie vines
allow a stolen kiss

Caffe dei Frari
Nini the white cat — tail up
strolls around with pride

shoes on St Marks Square
miss a slow crawling insect
unaware of danger

In the Venice mist
sightless forgotten mask eyes
scan a winter sky

Venice carnival
The Angel walks the high wire
upturned eyes mask fear

clutching tattered maps
Marco returns to old haunts
in Chinese slippers

stirring deep passion
as a moth is drawn to flame
love glides through Venice

walking with street map
searching for his mask workshop
she's lost in Venice

a soft summer light
foreshadows late night revels
when mask kisses mask

HAIKU OF ANCIENT FUTURES

Timeless Japanesque fragments of human interaction entwined with nature — sometimes delivered with a futuristic twist

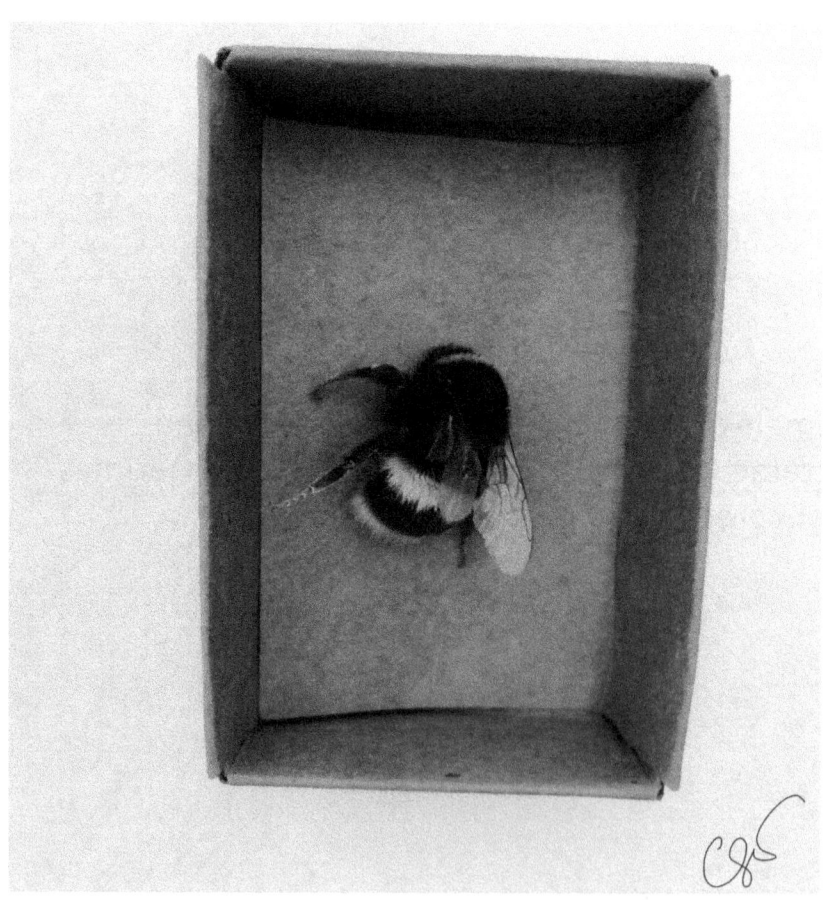

58

buzzing with nectar
bees are lost in honeyed thoughts
listening flowers nod

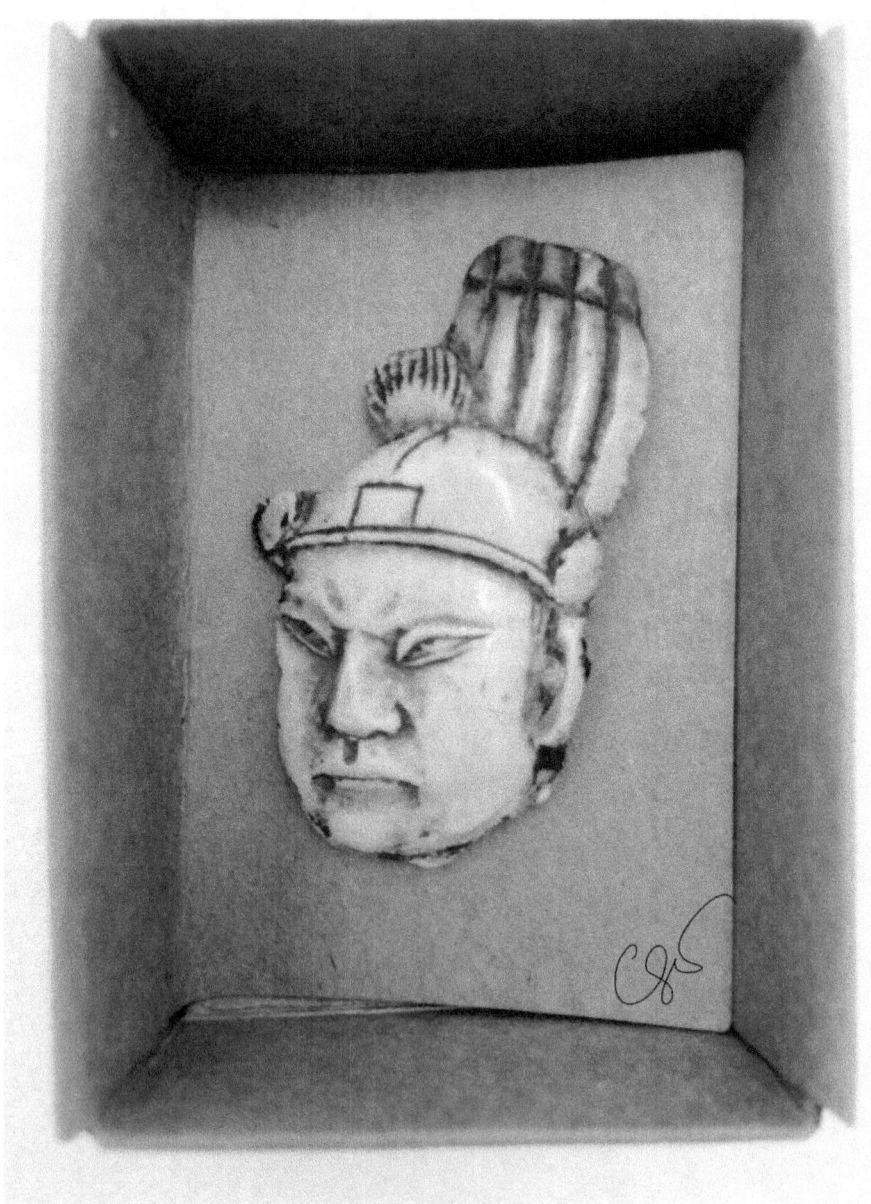

journeyman poet
searches for special places
to watch the moon rise

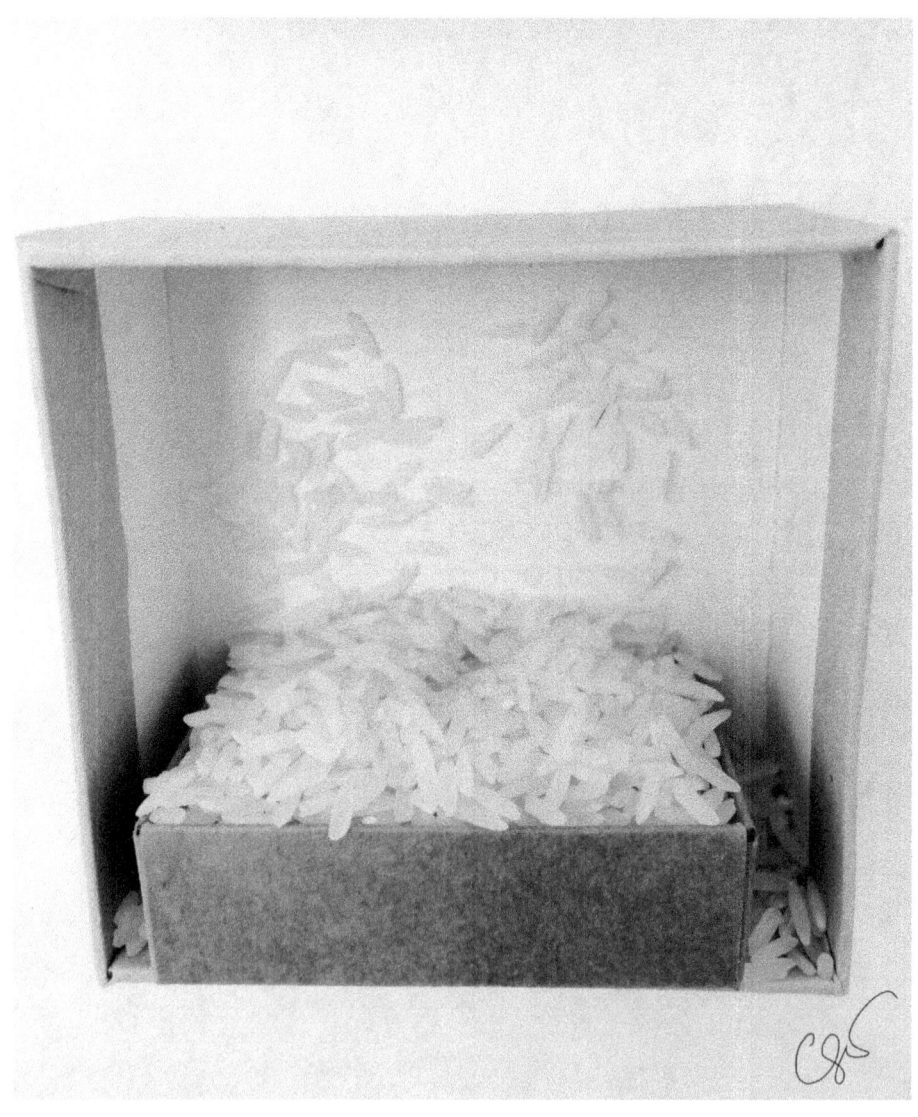

a drone brings us rice
before howling typhoon winds
tear at loose shutters

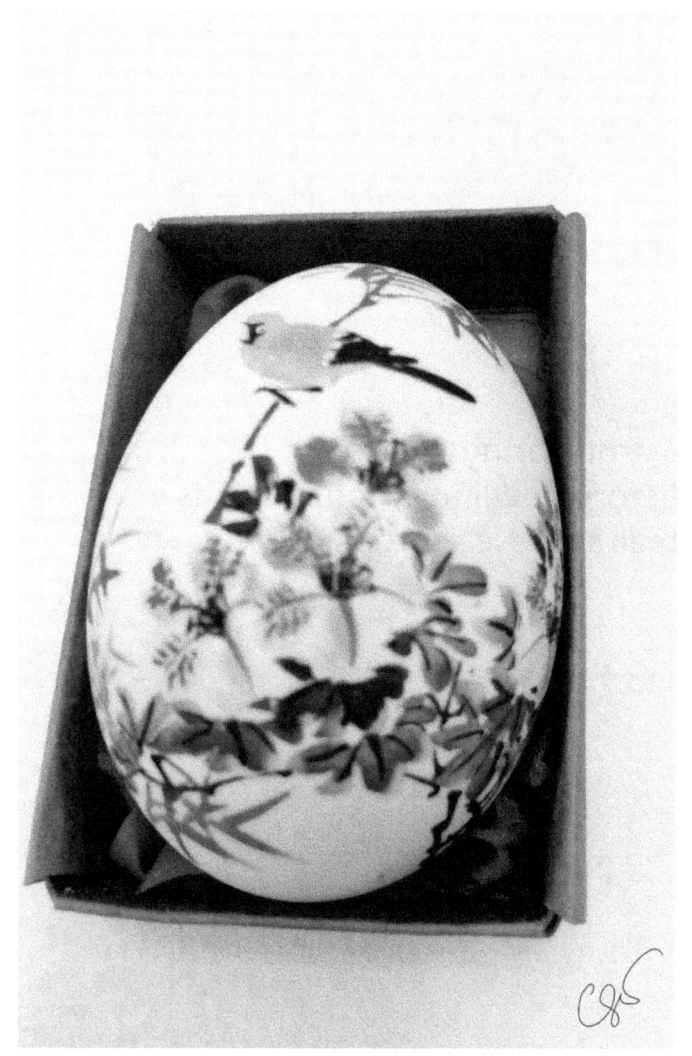

on the path in spring
one cold egg is found — it's sadness
changed with brush strokes

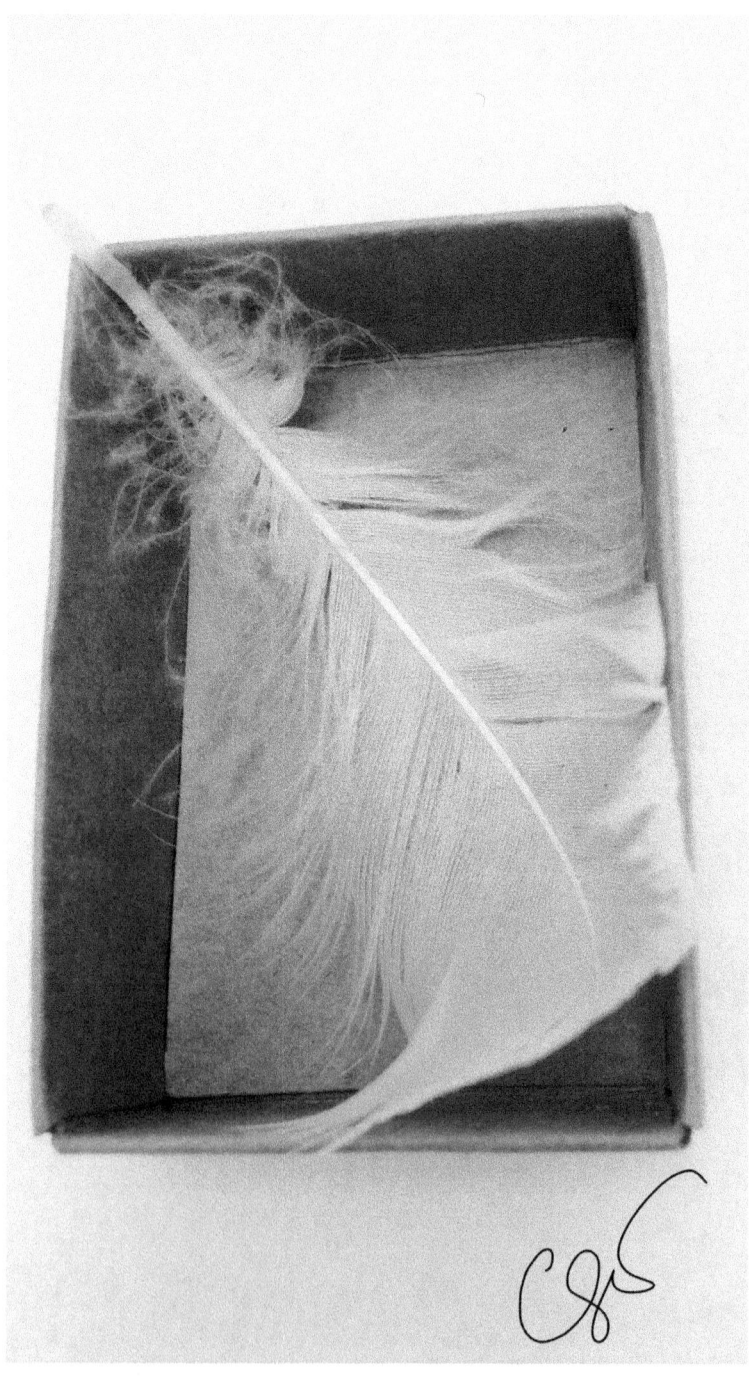

a small found feather
distant warbler in the wood
childhood stories float back

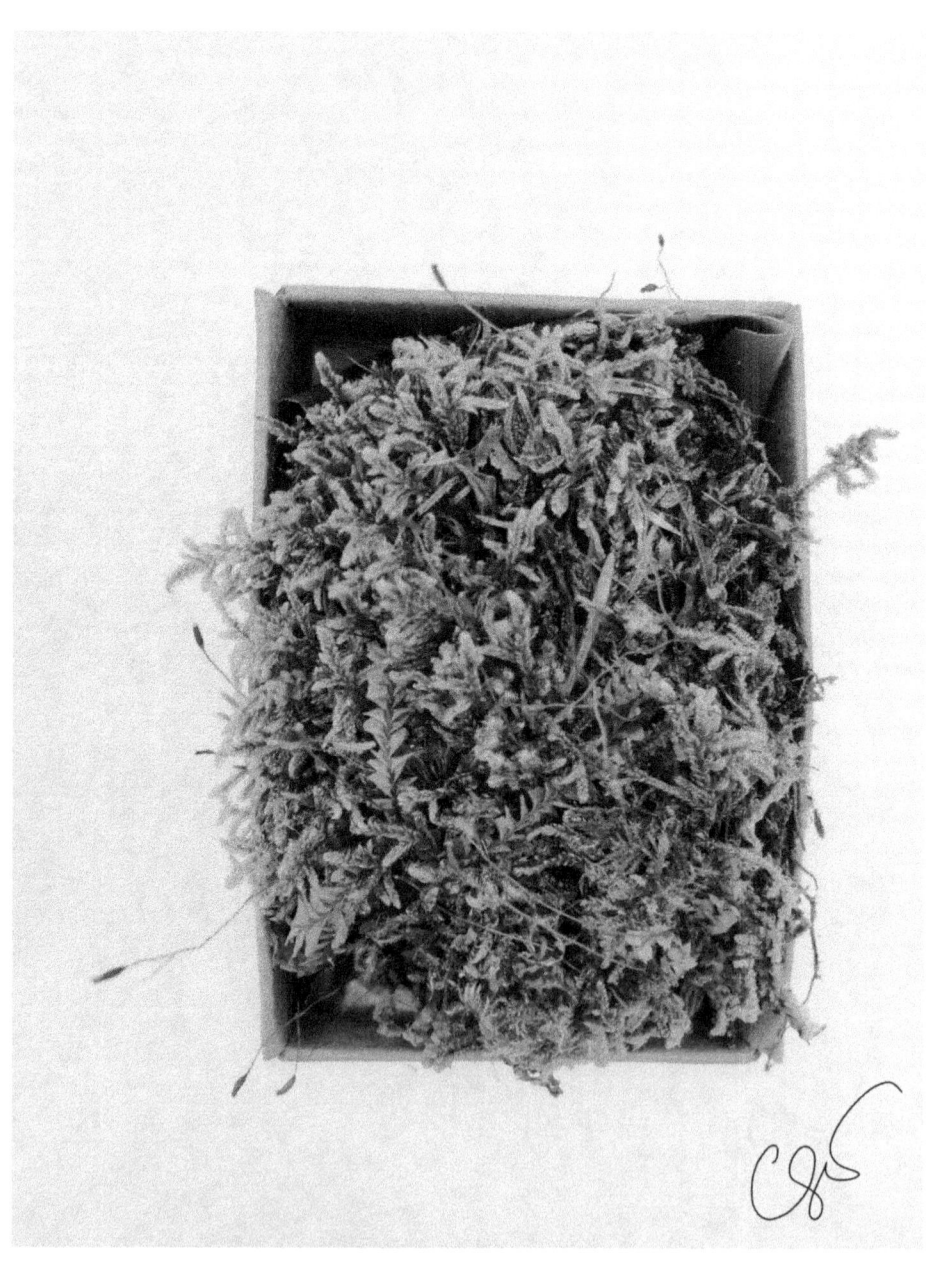

moss ancient as stone
sinks my feet in softest dew
as shadows retreat

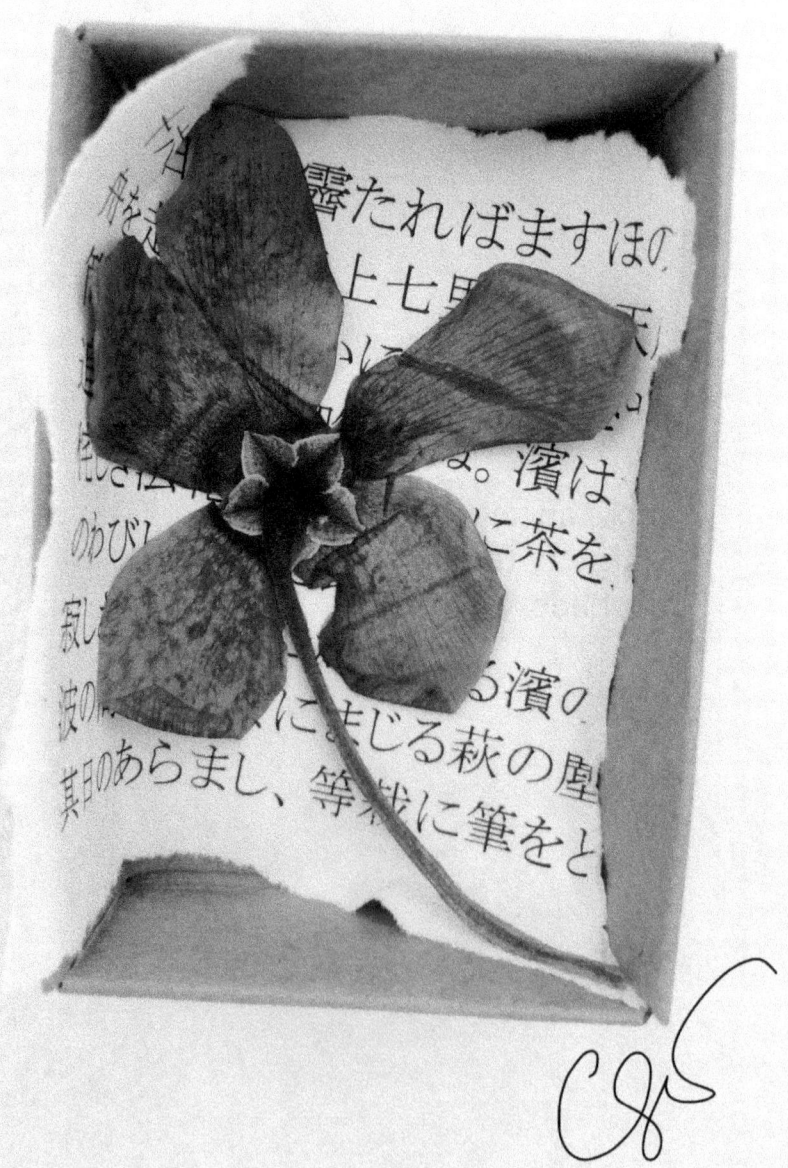

glowing summer flowers
pressed into flatness — are joy
 found in winter book

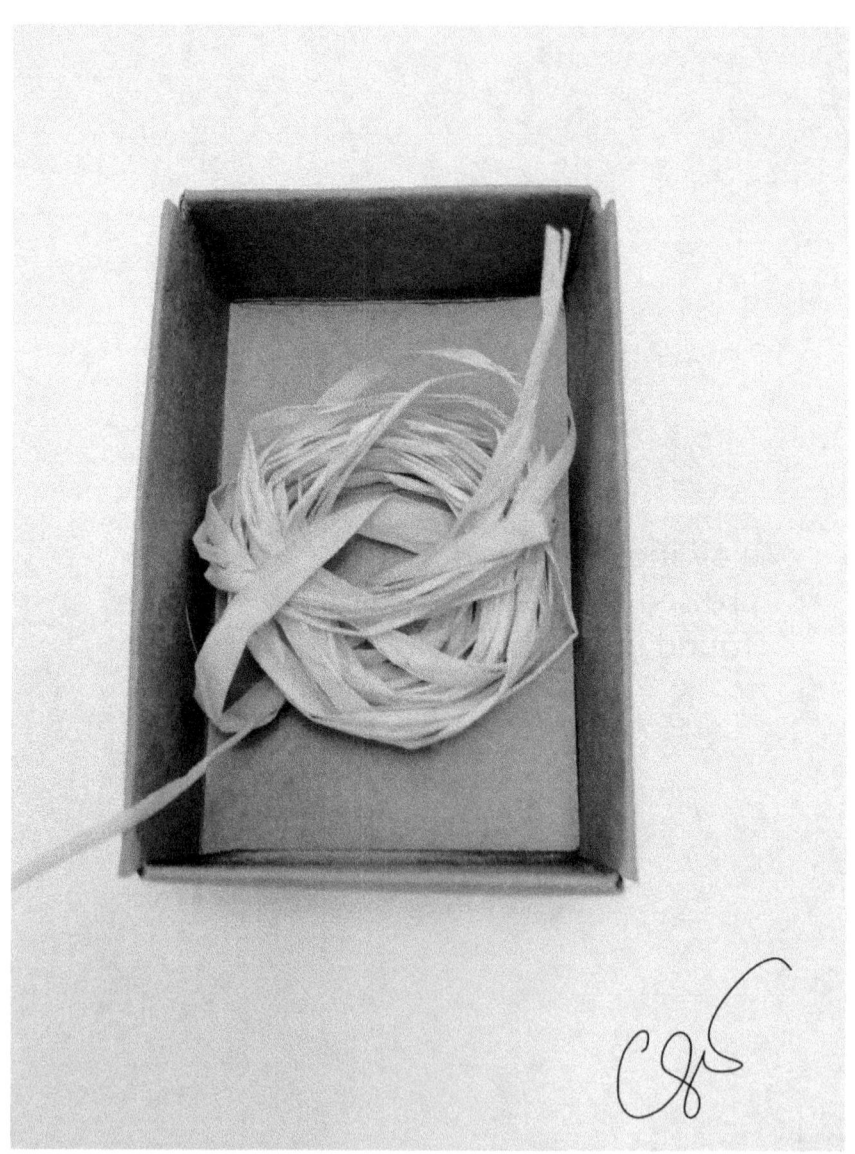

grass whispers — time to go
it bows low towards pathways
not chosen or planned

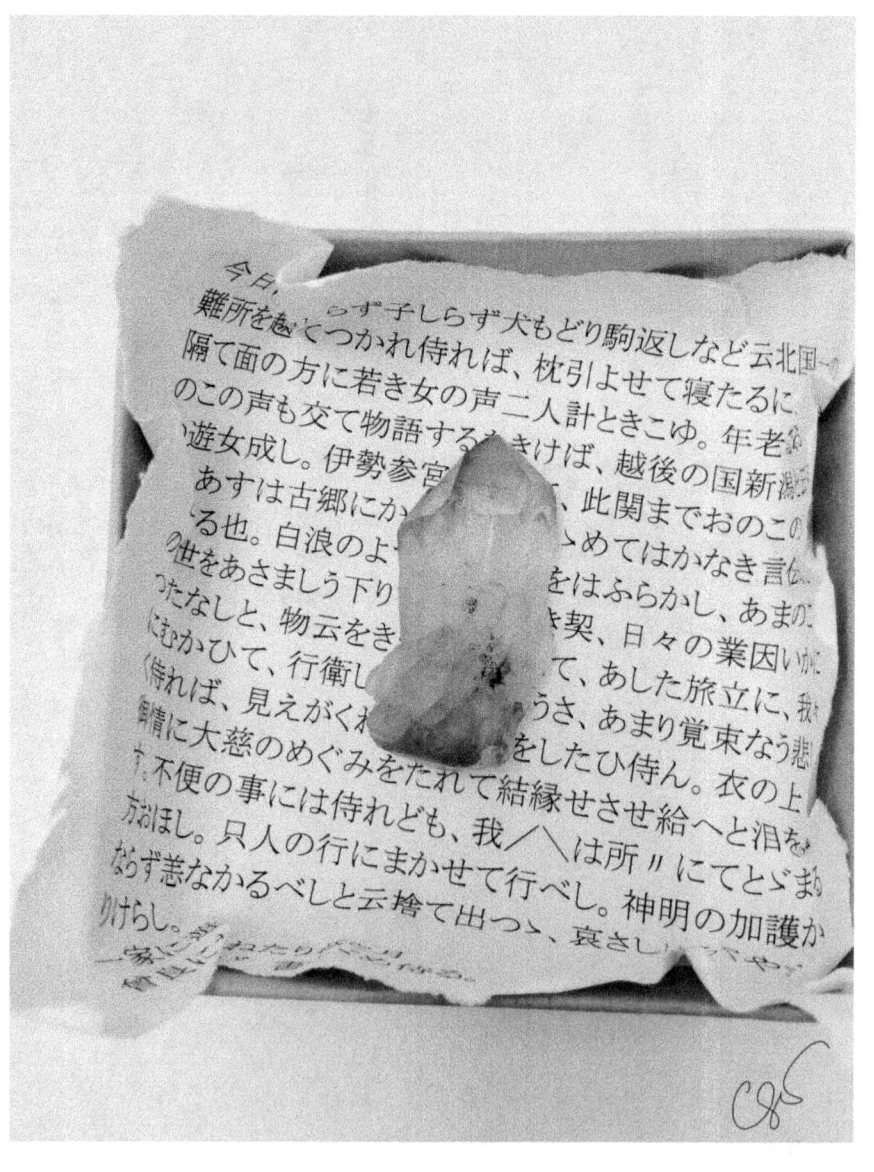

今日〈...〉〈...〉らず子しらず犬もどり駒返しなど云北国〈...〉
難所を〈...〉てつかれ侍れば、枕引よせて寝たるに
隔て面の方に若き女の声二人計ときこゆ。年老〈...〉
のこの声も交て物語するをきけば、越後の国新潟〈...〉
〈...〉遊女成し。伊勢参宮〈...〉、此関までおのこの〈...〉
あすは古郷にか〈...〉
〈...〉る也。白浪のよ〈...〉めてはかなき言伝〈...〉
〈...〉の世をあさましう下り〈...〉をはふらかし、あまの〈...〉
〈...〉つたなしと、物云をき〈...〉き契、日々の業因い〈...〉
〈...〉にむかひて、行衛し〈...〉て、あした旅立に、我〈...〉
〈...〉侍れば、見えがく〈...〉うさ、あまり覚束なう悲〈...〉
〈...〉情に大慈のめぐみをたれて結縁せさせ給へと泪を〈...〉
〈...〉不便の事には侍れども、我〳〵は所〃にてとどま〈...〉
〈...〉ほし。只人の行にまかせて行べし。神明の加護か〈...〉
〈...〉ならず恙なかるべしと云捨て出つゝ、哀さし〈...〉〈...〉や〈...〉
〈...〉けらし。

rainstorm cave shelter
yields lifelong crystal treasures
for candlelit winters

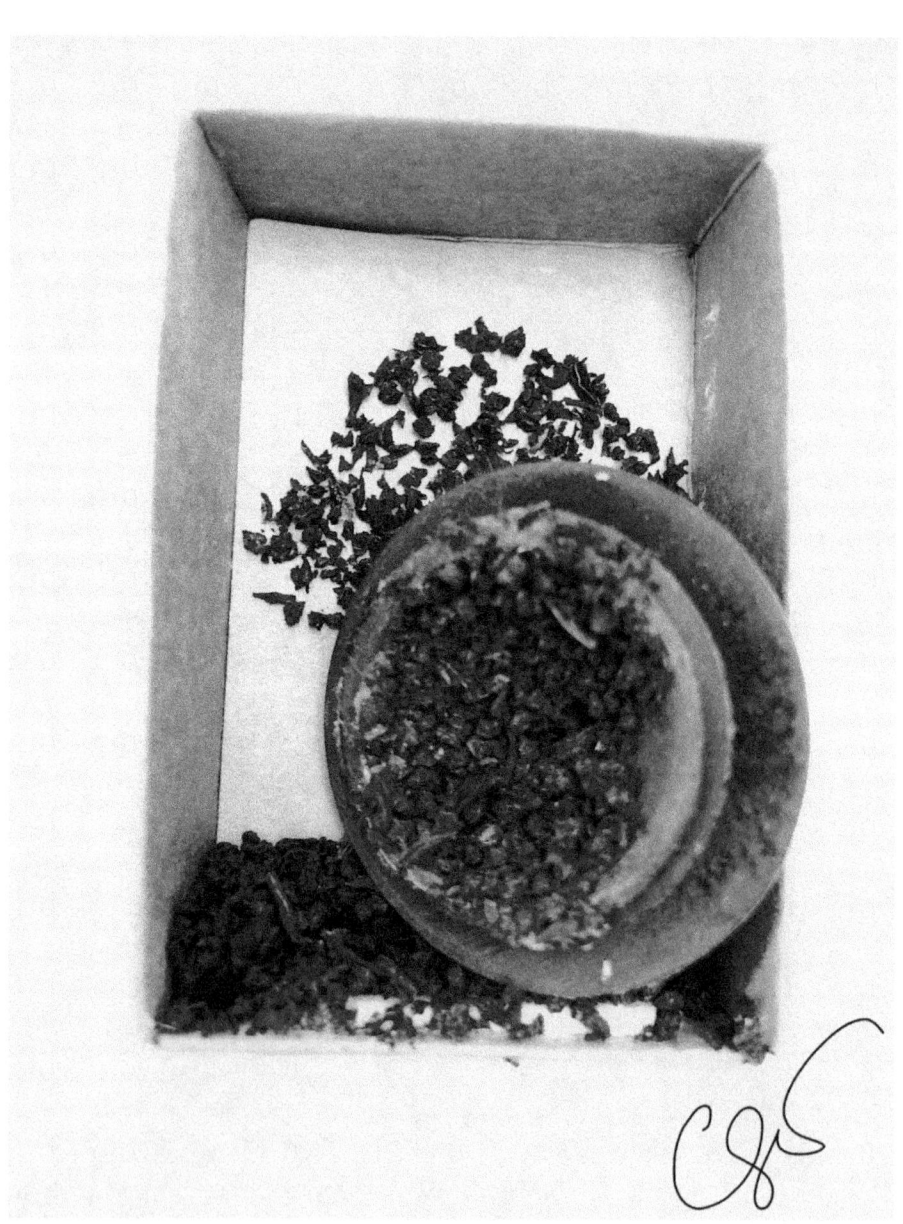

empty winter teahouse
holds ritual air — a breath
of ancient futures

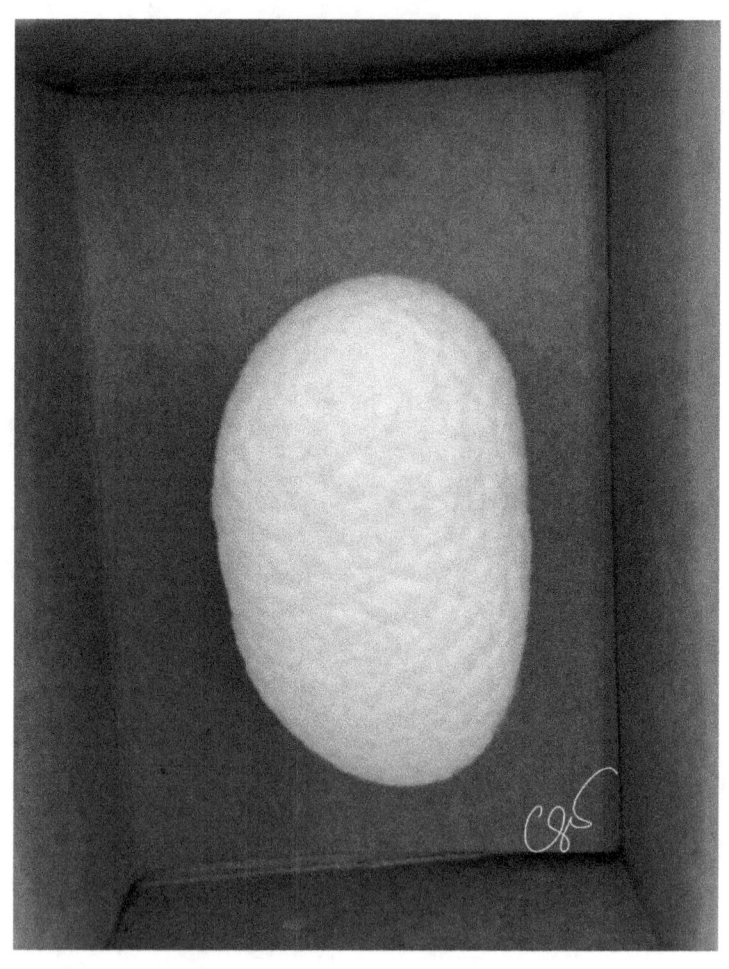

the silk worm cocoon
gives sensuous ritual sheen
to her geisha robe

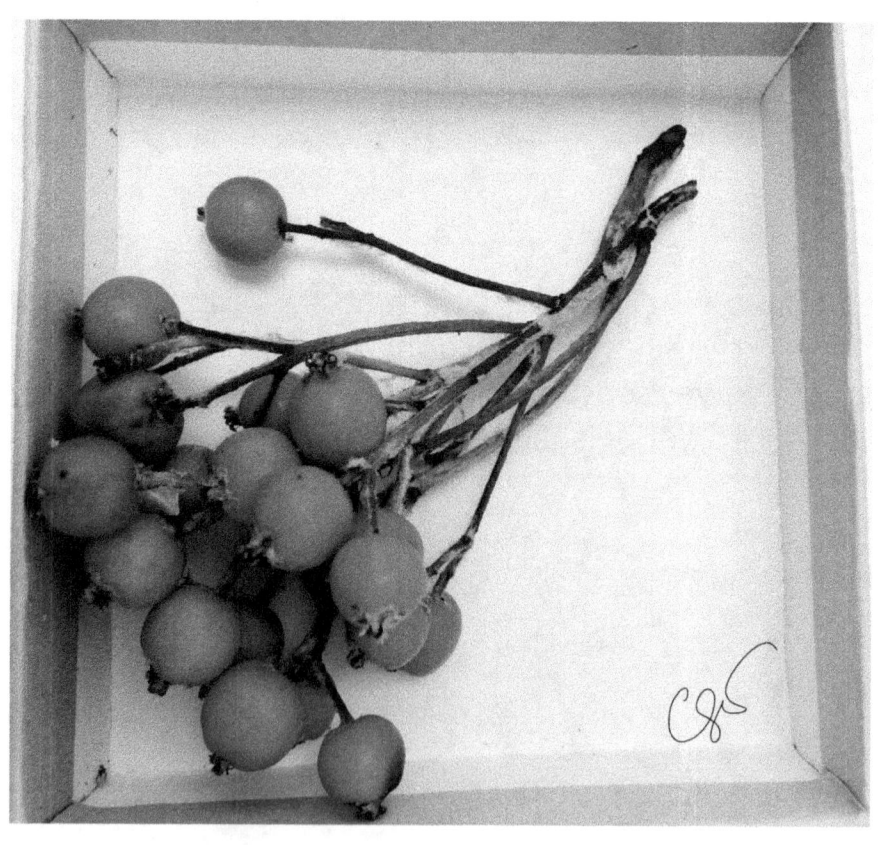

in late autumn sun
bright berries are gathered
for winter cordial

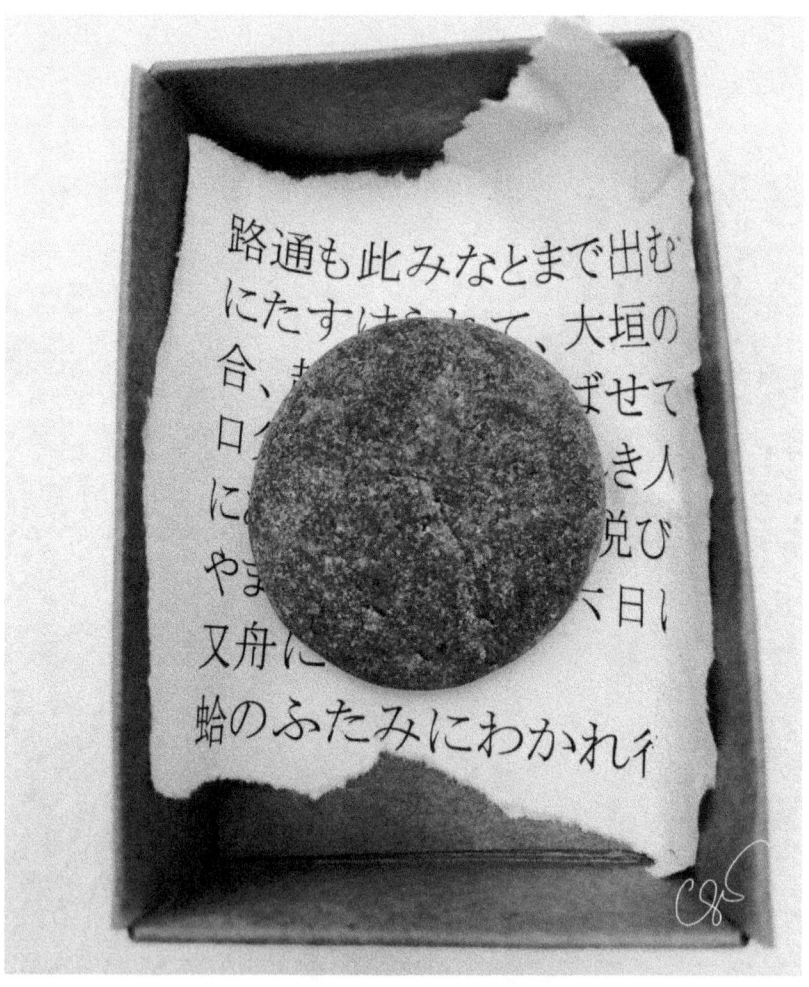

cicadas will not stop
a small boy lobs a round stone
and knows futility

Seventeen

sum of first 4 primes
wind chime poppies nod in time
Basho conducts tea

seventeen — her haiku year
now she knows everything
she is dangerous

Basho

journeyman poet
searches for special places
to watch the moon rise

the banana tree by the house
sustains him in sweetness
and gives him a name

Origins

when did haiku come
into the world — a garden
a wood — so many ways

when did boxes come
into the world a woman
a tree — so many ways

Basho and Okome　お米

straight as an arrow
the drone flies over blossom
to bring you a gift

quickly in summer
a small ring box is opened
shining eyes say yes

with strong winter eyes
he points to the evening star
and tells of clear skies

lying in the grass
birdsong lifts her tangled hair
a flower opens

winter's grip has melted
'it's here' — she cries — 'a map'
blossom floats on air

Bees

summers hum tickles grass
bee cud sweetens a child's mouth
into a wide-eyed smile

a bee staggers out
of a bright GM flower
the colony dies

bees strum summer strands
soft music brings memories
of honey sipped wine

sadly I bow low
to the dead bee on my path
my collection grows

Futures

a broken wing crane
falls to earth — undeterred a drone
continues southwards

frogs wait by the pool
a drone flies over — plop plop
koi carp disappear

a drone is lost
in floating mist a small box
awaits discovery

new man made birds fly
as forests slowly get forgotten
other worlds beckon

like a strange insect
the drone lands by my flowerpot
delivering a drop box

out of morning mist
drone insects land on a lily pads
surveying the scene

a dragonfly drone
flies the airbridge between us
bringing you presents

faraway a drone
falls to earth like a morning leaf
delivering pleasures

demented drones
skip drunkenly across the lake
their new controllers laugh

preprogrammed drones
searching to face-find people
hit trees — blossom falls

grey through a cloud mist
drone delivers hermit's rice
his stomach speaks a prayer

in distant mountains
a drone delivers rice cakes
thin monks bellies echo

on a high terrace
monks are silently listening
for deliverence

red leaves are falling
monks empty bowls are ready
scanning far horizons

it's too much trouble
planting rice — a box is drone-dropped
rice spills — grandma frowns

occasional rice drones
come from far distant worlds
where most are not thin

before drones landed
in an autumn forest glade
leaves were heard falling

a drone brings dry rice
before typhoon winds howl
and tear at shutters

a drone heralds change
skattering blossom cascades
pink petals around us

hovering over grasslands
the drone patrols a hidden temple
sounding out its depth

frogs flee landing drones
ripples on the cloud surface
disrupt calm water

Tea

tea sipped by the pond
watching a bright dragonfly
an air bridge between us

the empty teahouse
holds a deeply ritual air
of ancient futures

Neighbours

birdsong is scattered
when a drone flies over
bringing next doors gift

a peace offering
brought by wining drone in spring
sets our teeth on edge

Moss

moss ancient as stone
sinks my feet in softest dew
as shadows retreat

the old cracked pot pours
soft damp moss by the dew pond
a cushion for toads

mossed brokenness
an unexpected gift — the fence
creaks as deer push through

beside a moss path
a box has been delivered
I don't know what I ordered

bathing in summer
water spilling over moss
an old woman smiles

with silver sharp frost
humpback stones glow in moonlight
laced with moss shadow

Stone

when sandals are hole-y
every stone along the path
is felt by pilgrims

stone thrown into grass
disappears completely
my house waits empty

cicadas will not stop
a small boy lobs a stone
and knows futility

into the moon pond
a stone is thrown — the moon breaks
distant laughter heard

Silk

the silk worm cocoon
gives a soft sheen to her robe
in autumn evenings

Leaves

herald of autumn
the blood red leaf has fallen
a gauntlet at my feet

magic is stirring
yellow leaves fly up like birds
fungi caps begin to rise

Grass

grass whispers - time to go
it bends towards pathways
not chosen or planned

Pond

water-made — a low branch
drips sounds of spring
on a winter pond

Egg

on the path in spring
one cold egg is found
it's sadness changed with brush strokes

Nut

along the hut wall
a mouse roles a ginkgo nut
both will disappear

Japanese chipmunk
is certain with stored treasure
he will survive winter

Flower

glowing summer flowers
pressed into flatness — are joy
found in a winters book

Cold

the bamboo walking stick
in shadow by the door
has not moved since winter

loneliness as winds
wrap deep falling snow around
the old forest hut

now birds and water
fall silent — the mountain pass
is blocked till spring

the cool mountain mists
folds dawn in birdsong layers
of bamboo forest

Water

water falls a thousand feet
and scatters dancing rainbows
into upturned eyes

waterfalls are dry
whispered prayer lifts into sky
faces search for clouds

the leaking bucket
carried dripping along the way
gets lighter and grows sage

heavy dripping drops
in moon pond waters meeting
shiver with delight

Moon

moons hypnotic gaze
holds eyes too wide to be of use
in daylight

moon races half the night
with wind blown scudding clouds
and knows no rest

the lotus closes
as darkness falls — secretly
it opens in moonlight

water drips through moonlight
a moss curtain overhangs the rock
thirstily I squeeze

Crab

past bright tourist shops
and cars in shadow — a crab
must leave the sea its spawn

Crystal

rainstorm cave shelter
yields lifelong crystal treasures
for candlelight winters

Rice

rice steams in a bowl
a wooden chair upturned
tells a broken story

the empty home creaks
the sake was spilled long ago
the dry stain lingers

each paddy field is tended
by generations who know
the value of rice

Walking stick

glad of my stick
that was one step ahead
I followed

Gardens

dew dances over grass
in one hundred thousand suns
my sleeve is wet with tears

web designed by spider
is beauty spun across the path
I walk another way

dry poppy heads rattle
in autumn — upended red dancing skirts
are futures past

blossom drifts across the terrace
confetti drifts across the grass
the bride left long ago

immense distance filled
between frog croaking
and distant calling bird

Woods

small found feather
distant warbler in the wood
childhood stories float back

strands of birdsong
drift through bamboo forests
a cat dreams on a shelf

poured through an open window
sunshine and wood sounds
a distant cuckoo marks time

haiku fall like autumn leaves
as I walk the tree lined path
wind wrapped

ancient bamboo forest
light bars filter - pandas slowly chew
drone's shadow slices the air

there were few sunny clearings
on my forest journey
I thought there would be more

searching for ink-caps
haikus and leaves float through air
with scent of autumn

basket full of fungi
pungent with aromatic promise
of soup and black ink

picked one afternoon
gathered for winter cordial
bright autumn berries

like the growing snake
the tree sheds it's skin
bark drops on the path

Home

carp keeps water clean
they swarm and churn for rice cake
and wash our plates

in storm light
distant thunder roles — a loose shutter bangs
it needs a nail

liquid light pours
onto the terrace bathed in light
I dive in and float

from journeying
through mountain passes
only one blister remains

frost delights my winter path
at first bare blue feet recoil
from biting cold

frosted sparkling ice
brings childhood necklace memories
to my winter pond

winter cold steams on thatch
starlight jewels in frosted air
smoke reaches into branches

winter storms have raged
but strong bamboo makes easy
repairs to my roof

Art

birch bark peels and scrolls
I reach for the black cap ink and brush
poems come on the breeze

from soft brush of ink
thought threads are pictured gestures
held in earth moments

pond stilled reflection
laughs with rain drops sometimes
spreading circle waves

torn maps float up on fire
high into damp autumn sky
their pathways lost to earth

spring — span of brushed ink
wings glide above with sharp eyes
seeing many sky-paths

imaginations
high strong bridge arcs wind-blown space
between more solid ground

HAIKU: A GARDEN

Moments of life from spring days
in Aldeburgh Sensory Garden

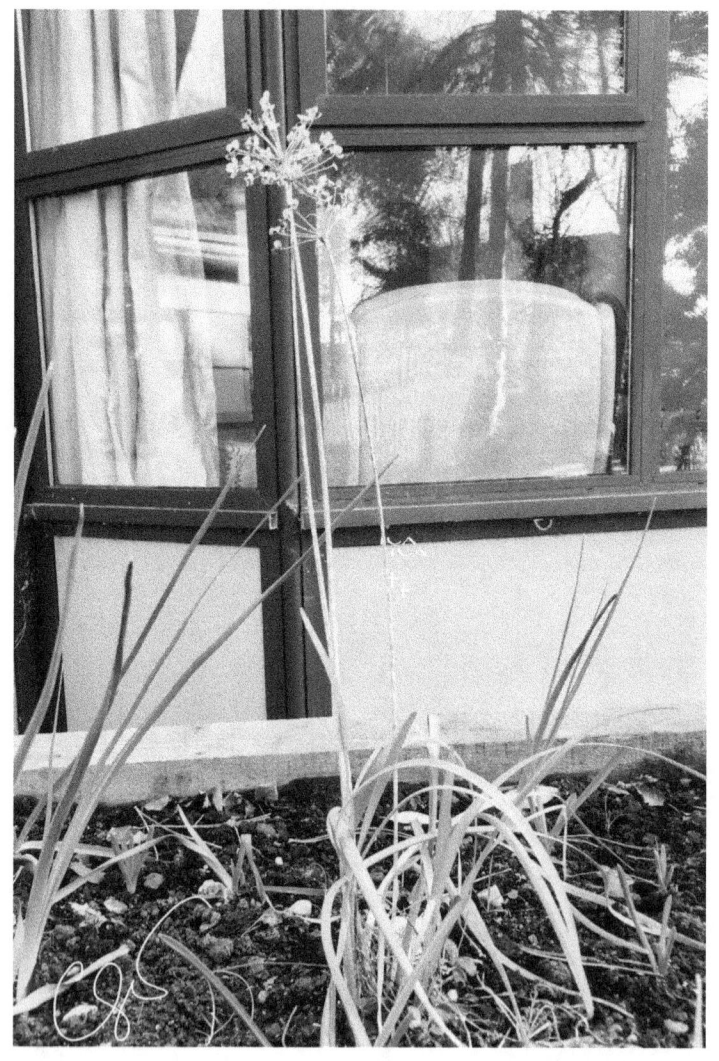

sensory gardens
soft notes whisper in grasses
stroking gentle breeze

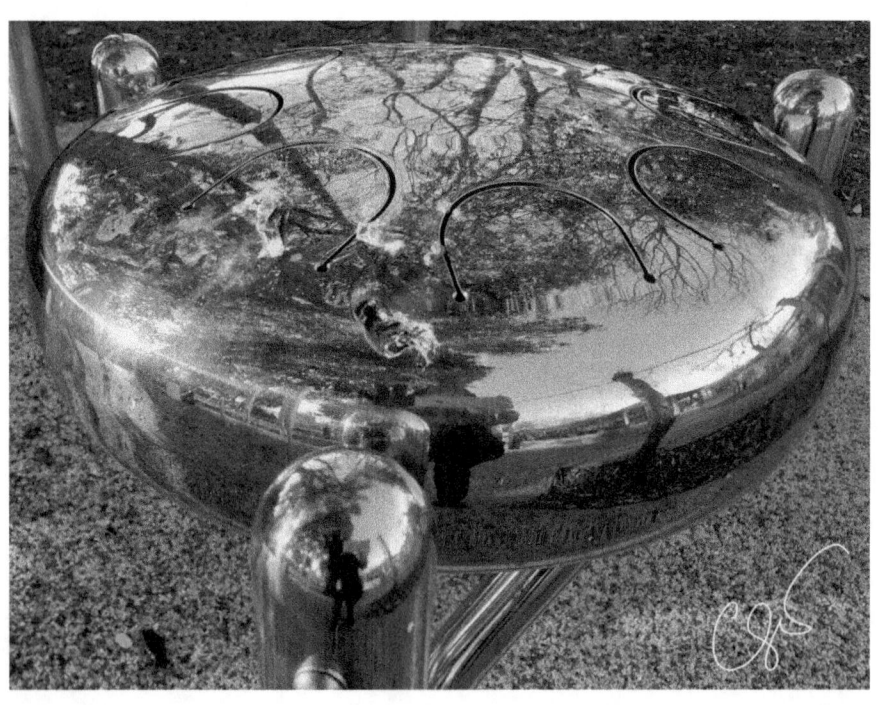

bird poo splattering
ideas of musical fun
or silent reflection

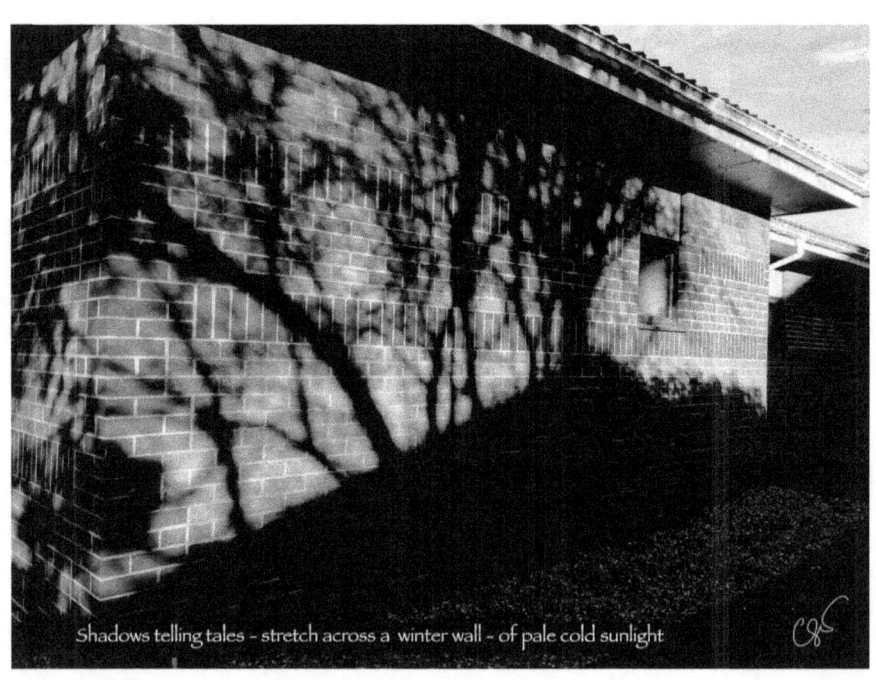

Shadows telling tales – stretch across a winter wall – of pale cold sunlight

shadows telling tales
stretch across a winter wall
in pale cold sunlight

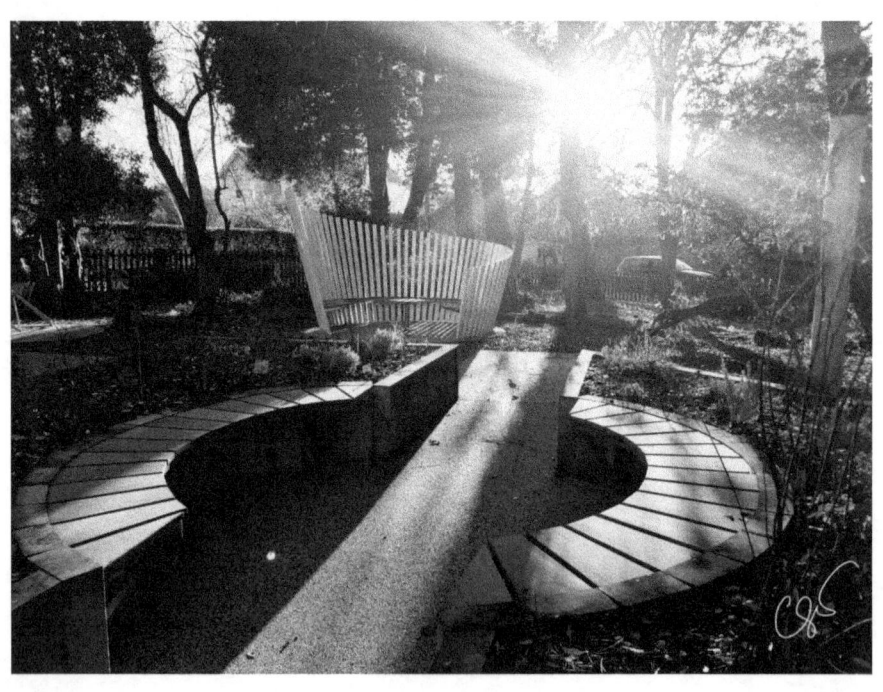

rest with flower beds
sun splatters the curling bench
beneath the branches

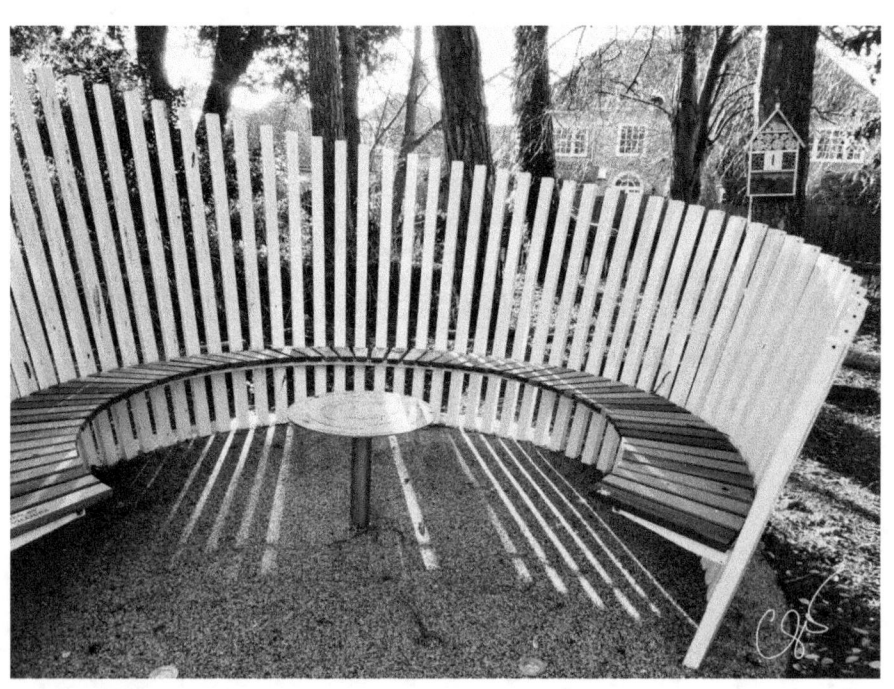

nesting box above
the yellow bench spring colours
bringing healing light

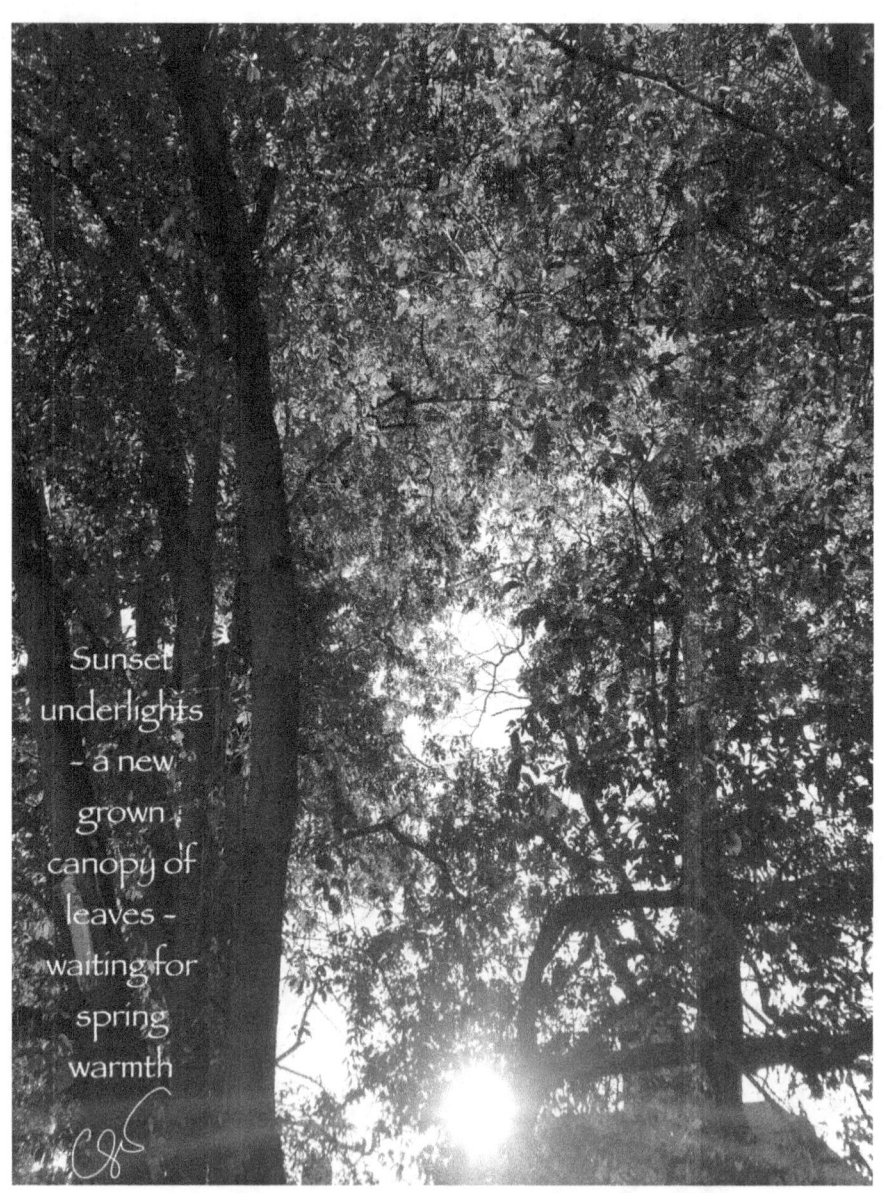

Sunset
underlights
– a new
grown
canopy of
leaves –
waiting for
spring
warmth

122

sunset under-lights
a new grown canopy of leaves
waiting for spring warmth

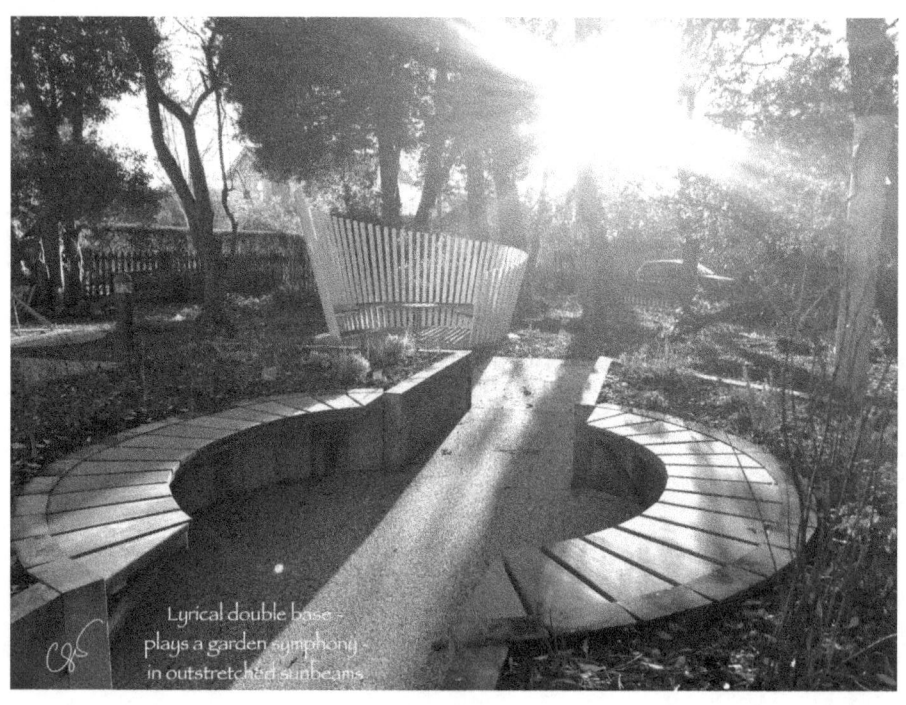

Lyrical double base -
plays a garden symphony -
in outstretched sunbeams

lyrical double bass
plays a garden symphony
for outstretched sunbeams

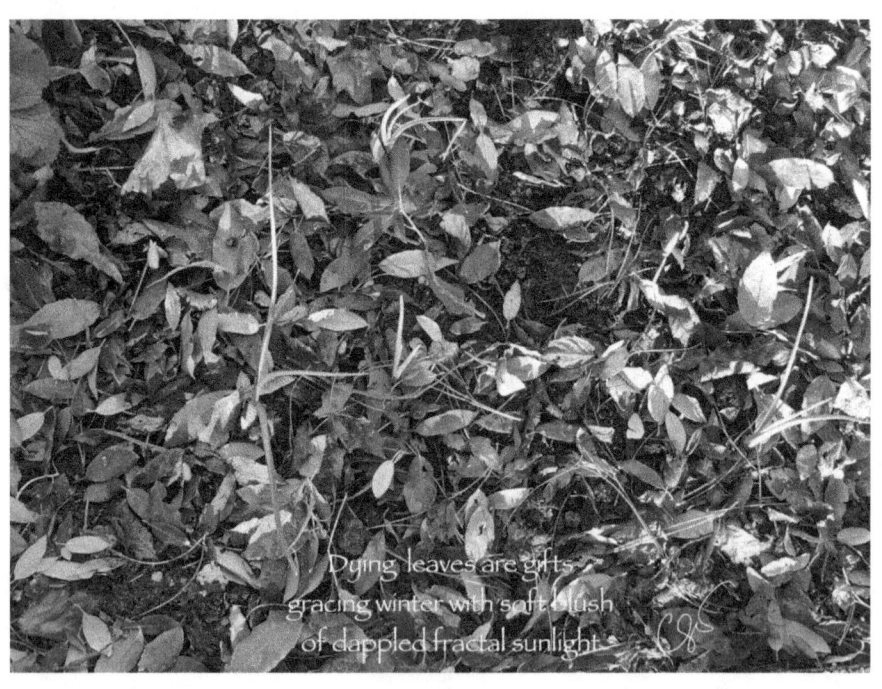

Dying leaves are gifts
gracing winter with soft blush
of dappled fractal sunlight

dying leaves are gifts
gracing winter with soft blush
of dappled sunlight

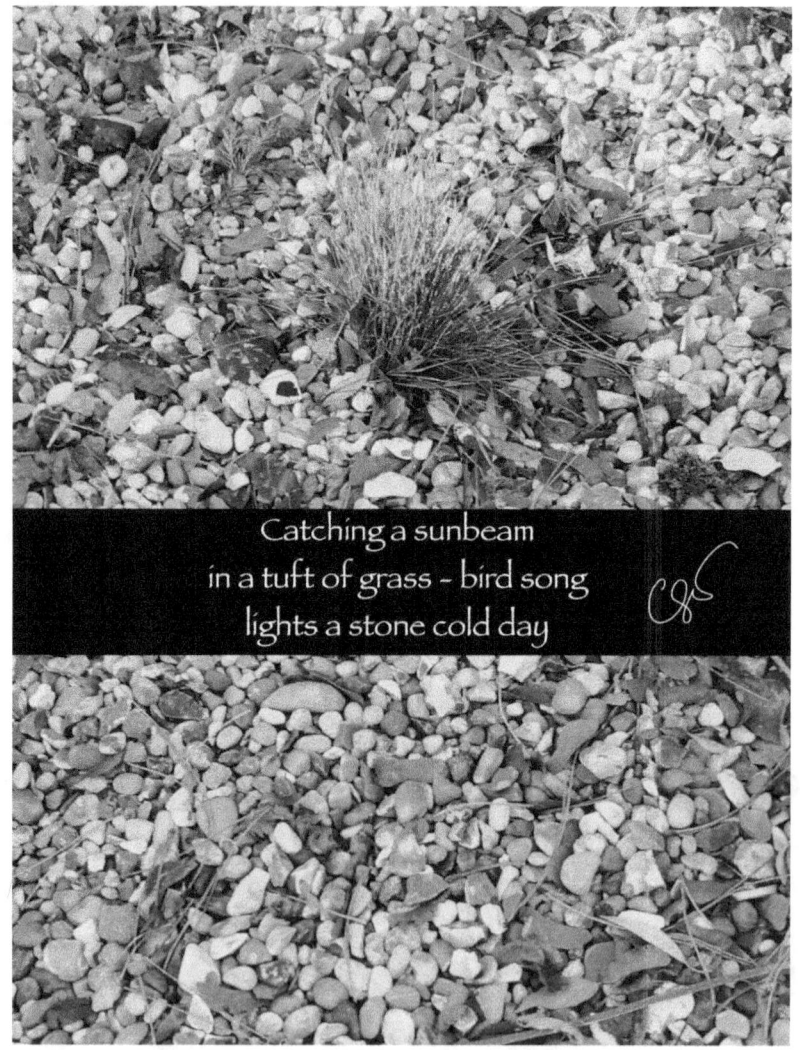

Catching a sunbeam
in a tuft of grass - bird song
lights a stone cold day

catching a sunbeam
in a tuft of grass — bird song
lights a stone cold day

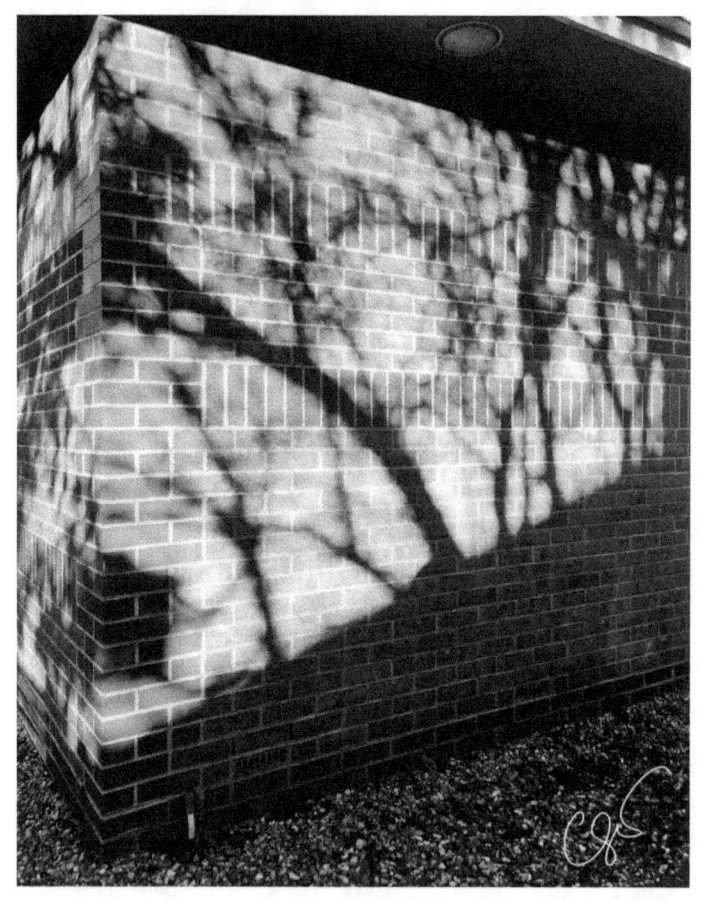

shadow puppet dance
of branches in light spring breeze
earth waits for warmth

sensory gardens notes
are whispered sounds of flowers
in softly blowing breeze

sensory garden
listening to leafy branches
gently brushed by air

drink in the garden
plants draw up earth's water
deeply felt well being

beneath the music of leaves
a garden symphony
unfolds in time

a seed burst unwraps
reaching up towards the light
pushing earth aside

mindfully with infinite patience
the season turned
the garden over

a garden space
here touch a moment's pleasure
to sit in sun splashed air

www.ingramcontent.com/pod-product-compliance
Lightning Source LLC
Chambersburg PA
CBHW071443180526
45170CB00001B/440